What people are

Hope Rising: Finding Hope in a Turbulent World

"Markets will rise and fall. Wealth will be gained and lost. But the hope that rises from our Lord will endure forever. My thanks to Ben Foley and Lars Dunberg for sharing their unique perspective from decades of ministry in the trenches."

—Tony Amaradio
Coauthor, *Faithful with Much*; philanthropist; CEO, Select Portfolio Management

"Hope is a universal need and a deep cry of every human heart. As followers of Jesus, we have endless access to the source of all lasting hope both for ourselves and to share with the world in our own unique ways as image-bearers of God. Ben Foley and Lars Dunberg have written a timely book that all generations can benefit from!"

—Mark Batterson
New York Times best-selling author, *The Circle Maker*; Lead Pastor of National Community Church

"*Hope Rising* comes to us in a season filled with uncertainty: a pandemic, nation-wide racial division, and economic and political unrest. Ben and Lars provide us with a biblical response of hope. Through real-life testimonials from Bible heroes, this book is both timely and timeless. It grants us a fresh glimpse of God's love for His people in action. Jesus Christ is the hope of the world, and you and I are being invited to be a part of the God-story of the World, and you and I can be part of His God story."

—Dr. Wayne Cordeiro
President, New Hope Christian College; senior pastor, New Hope West; founder Master of Arts in Formational Leadership; author

"I have competed internationally with Ben Foley for many years on rugged Sports Evangelism ministries in Latin America. Ben's gifted insight on hope and real-life experiences expressed in his writings will help many Christians find comfort, clarity, and joy through life's disappointments and turmoil."

—David Gordon
President, Sport X Change

"Right now, we are in desperate need of hope! Thankfully, in the midst of global turbulence and disruption, hope is on the rise. This book shares the story of *ServeNow*, but even more significantly, Ben tells a story that anchors us in hope and opens our eyes to where God is on the move. Inspiring!"

—Peter Greer
President and CEO, HOPE International

"In a world that is driven by the madness of the news cycle, we could really use an infusion of hope right now. And *Hope Rising* might just be the thing you need. It's filled with vivid stories of what God is doing through his people all over the earth. Grab this book and read it."

—Daniel Grothe
Pastor and author, *Chasing Wisdom*

"There is no more needed anchor on life's turbulent seas than 'hope.' Ben Foley and Lars Dunberg, veterans of international and personal ministry, have crafted stories of hope based in scripture and personified through life circumstances to remind us of a God who exhibits his care throughout the valleys and mountaintops of life—bringing us back to hope."

—Tim Gunsolley
President and CEO, Elevation Growth Partners

"Every time you turn on the television, open the front page of the newspaper, or glimpse that feed from Apple News, you are inundated with 'bad news.' From COVID, forest fires, storms, riots, and stock market crashes, now more than ever stories of Hope are not only needed but are necessary. Ben and Lars do not candy coat the harsh realities but instead articulate how our God of Hope is with us in our suffering. *Hope Rising* is anchored in the biblical view of Hope through the lives of Jacob, Joseph, and Paul to name a few who have found Hope amid their struggles. These, along with real life testimonials, will lift your spirits, help you to think differently, and to live life on purpose because of our God of Hope."

—Dr. Guy Higashi
Director online and graduate programs, New Hope Christian College; program manager Master of Arts in Formational Leadership, Capital Seminary

"Some people think that to be hopeful—especially in today's messy environment—is naïve or even silly. Not these two authors. With clear eyes and a solid reliance on the One who sees all, knows all, and is not at all nervous, they map out the realistic way to peace and hope-filled living. Read this book, take a deep breath, and then move ahead with confidence."

—Dean Merrill
Publishing executive and award-winning author

"Filled with stories, wisdom and encouragement harvested from decades of Gospel mission, *Hope Rising* delivers an all-access playbook to rediscover a God that is bigger and better than anything we could ever imagine—or hope."

—Geof Morin
CEO, Biblica/The International Bible Society

"Hope Rising is an amazing and timely book. The subtitle is very descriptive: "Finding Hope in a Turbulent World." We live in uncertain and anxiety-producing times. Young and old are searching for hope in a seemingly hopeless world.

"Ben Foley, with his esteemed coauthor, Lars Dunberg, offers practical wisdom for getting through the storms of life. Ben shares real-life lessons from people who've endured death, disease, loss, disappointment, and tragedy. The book teaches how to turn setbacks from bitterness to strength and healing.

"There are no promises of an easy road. But God works in the background to give us practical hope when the world around you is falling apart. We read biblical and global examples of the truth of Romans 8:28.

"Hope Rising is well-written, biblically-based and life-applicable. Highly recommended."

—Wayne Pederson
Global Ambassador

"Hope Rising what an appropriate title for your book. Your work through *ServeNow* has greatly enlarged God's Kingdom. Thank you for allowing Cynthia and me to participate with you in God's Master Plan of seeing 'His Word covers the earth as the waters cover the sea.'"

—Mike Richards
Former Chair, Biblica/International Bible Society

"Romans 5:5 promises that 'hope does not disappoint,' and neither does this book! I've known Ben Foley since he was a teenager. I've admired his passion for Jesus and his commitment to global mission. Watching his faithfulness through the years has given me great hope for the next generation of church leadership. In a culture that "crosses their fingers" with shallow hope, Ben has given us a depth of hope anchored in the Word of God."

—Rich Stevenson
Director, The Malachi Network

"Life inevitably creates moments—seasons even—where it's easy and normal to feel void of hope. This book is a terrific, inspirational reminder that hope for today, and a hope that endures, exists in a personal relationship with Jesus and is supported by the truth(s) of God's Word. What a great call to all to 'Not lose heart!'"

—Greg Stoughton
Partnership and project coordinator, Office of the President, Cru

"Even from his early years at Lancaster Bible College, it was evident my friend Ben Foley would lead with humility and significantly. His tome *Hope Rising: Finding Hope in a Turbulent World* arrives at a most unique intersection in human history where chaos seems to loom at every corner despite our technological advances and unparalleled prosperity. His thoughtful reflections on hope, led by the Author of all hope, will both challenge and encourage you for our current reality, and the days ahead."

—Dr. Peter W. Teague
President Emeritus, Lancaster Bible College | Capital Seminary & Graduate School

"The world has never needed hope more than it does today. That is what this book is about and why it is needed so badly. Ben Foley and Lars Dunberg are uniquely qualified to write a book such as this. Because of their biblical training and many years of service in global ministries, they have their finger on the pulse of the world's greatest needs while also possessing a depth of theological knowledge to provide profound answers to those needs. I strongly commend this book to anyone looking for hope in these dark days!"

—Rick Thompson
President, Global Action

"This book is for you! In contrast to previous generations, the present and upcoming generations have never experienced such a dramatic chapter in the history of humanity. The global lockdowns created personal uncertainty, discouragement, confusion, despair, distrust, and even death. A senior leader, Lars Dunberg and an emerging leader, Ben Foley, are making quite an impact around the world with *ServeNow*. In this book they combine their biblical convictions, their personal experiences, and the stories of real people whom in the midst of real tragedies, disappointments, and unexpected crisis found the real hope that the whole world desperately needs. That is what this book is all about. If you love stories of real people finding real hope, then this book is for you!"

—Galo Vasquez
VELA Ministries International, Mexico

"Think all hope is lost in these turbulent times? Think again! Drawing on their personal experiences and biblical truth, Ben Foley and Lars Dunberg inspire us with examples of hope. But they don't stop there, challenging us to also provide hope to others. A timely message for us all!"

—Emily Voorhies
Founder, Tirzah International

"There could not be a better time than the present to build hope in the hearts of men and women worldwide. I'm so thankful for ministries such as *ServeNow* as they spread the love of Jesus Christ around the globe in real, tangible, heartfelt ways. Thank you, Lars and Ben, for writing such a timely and much needed book."

—Marcos Witt
Pastor; author; Grammy Award winning artist; founder, CanZion Group

HOPE RISING

Finding hope in a turbulent world

BEN FOLEY
WITH LARS B. DUNBERG

Hope Rising: Finding Hope in a Turbulent World

By Ben Foley with Lars B. Dunberg
Copyright © 2020 by *ServeNow*. All rights reserved.

ISBN 978-1-952186-55-4

Published by *ServeNow*, 1817 Austin Bluffs Parkway, #110, Colorado Springs, CO 80918.

Dedicated to Steve and Kristen Manz.
It was Steve who told us that
what *ServeNow* gives him is

HOPE.

Turbulent–

A turbulent time, place, or relationship is one in which there is a lot of change, confusion, and disorder. (Collins: British English)

Table of Contents

Acknowledgments

This is my first time writing a complete book. I had no real idea the amount of work and people involved that go into bringing a book into reality! Writing the content was the easy part. The hard part was all the many little details that followed.

Therefore, I want to take a moment to thank some key people. First, I want to thank one of my mentors, Rich Stevenson, who kept encouraging me to become an author. Second, I want to thank Lars Dunberg, not only for coauthoring this book, but also spending an enormous amount of time working with me back and forth on various thoughts, ideas, and details that go into publishing a book. Many conversations and late nights were spent, and I always marvel at his seemingly endless supply of energy and enthusiasm!

Third, I want to thank Marianne Hering for her editing work and attention to detail, which is not one of my strongest points! She has made my writing more succinct and clearer than it really is. Fourth, I want to thank Paul Dunberg, who spent hours typesetting this book. Fifth, I want to thank Peter Schmidt who worked with us on the design for the book, and Mike and Chris King for their help with the printing aspects. These are all colleagues who have collaborated together on other projects through the years as well and with whom I am privileged to share this journey of faith!

I also want to sincerely thank the board at *ServeNow* who fully embraced not only this book concept but also generously gave above and beyond of their own resources to help cover production costs! I am also so thrilled with the number of people willing to write an endorsement and put their name behind it in support of seeking to provide hope to those most in need.

Additionally, thank you to all of those people who allowed me to share their personal stories in this book to illustrate how hope is rising around the world. I am also grateful to all those who partner with *ServeNow* and have been praying for this whole process. It is because of those prayers that this book is a reality, and I believe it will be those prayers that will cause this book to get into the hands of those who need it most at a divinely appointed time.

Last, but not least, I have to thank my lovely and supportive wife, Lauren! She allowed me the time and space to devote to this book on top of everything else. I know I take her quiet and consistent actions behind the scenes for granted more than I should. Perhaps the best compliment I can give her is that she has the strength of her two grandmothers!

It brings me great joy to know that no royalties will go to either authors, but all proceeds and profit from the sale of this book will directly go back into *ServeNow* to continue fulfilling our mission in *sharing Christ's passion for the world by serving the most vulnerable through national churches and leaders.* The example of our leaders and partners around the world continue to inspire, motivate, and bring tremendous levels of hope to my own heart and life!

Preface

Why a book on hope? If there is one thing the world needs more than anything else, it's hope.

Hope became a focus for me when my wife, Lauren, and I named our second daughter Alexis Hope. Her birth, along with that of our first daughter, Ava Marie, was the fulfillment of the hope and desire I had to one day have daughters. Our two boys, Maximus and Rocky, are the fulfillment of Lauren's hope and desire to have boys. The children remind us of God's faithful promise of hope amid a world that often feels overwhelmingly hopeless.

I dedicated this book to Steve and Kristen Manz because it was during a conversation with them that Steve articulated hope in a way that profoundly struck me. That was also the moment I had a vision to write a book on hope together with my mentor and *ServeNow*'s founder, Lars Dunberg.

While I am the primary author, I asked Lars to write chapters 4 and 8 exclusively. Chapter 4 is the origin story of *ServeNow*, which he founded alongside his daughter Maria Sturt. To me, it's a story of hope, because it arose out of utter hopelessness. I asked Lars to write chapter 8 because he has spent much of his life dedicated to getting God's Word translated and in the hands of people around the world. He has seen the power of God's Word provide hope to countless millions worldwide who experience hopelessness in myriad ways. He and I deeply believe that if the world's people, including those in the United States, are going to rediscover hope, then we need to rediscover God's Word, which is a book full of hope.

I have been an avid reader all my life, and I love to write. I have dreamed and carried within me the hope of writing books. This book is a testament of God's power as we put our hope in the one true source and provider of all good things: Jesus Christ, the hope of the world.

Ben Foley
Colorado Springs
November 1, 2020

1

When All Hope Seems Lost

"Everything is against me!"
—Jacob, Genesis 42:36

Chad Barrett recently asked me to endorse a book he is writing called *Thrive, Not Just Survive.* It's the true story of his battle with anxiety and depression, the loss of his young daughter, Kristina, to cancer, and other disappointments—both personal and in ministry—he has faced. He opens the first chapter with this statement:

> God gives us more than we can handle, but he doesn't give us a worthless trial. Going through storms of life can be painful to bear, of course. But the real darkness exists in a lack of trust in the sovereign God whose love is indescribable and power unfathomable.[1]

Like my friend Chad, we all go through seasons and situations where life seems hopeless and even God himself appears to be against us. In fact, this book does not promise that if you just have enough hope you will be spared difficult situations, protected from all pain, or have all your dreams come true. This book does not promise that if you just follow a certain formula, your marriage will be perfect, your children will all turn out as you desire, or that all your relationships will be restored. Instead, the stories in this book show that when everything collapses, hope can rise from the ashes.

Hope rises in my New Jersey church

When I was 25 years old, I began learning about this kind of hope while pastoring a church in New Jersey. During that six-year period, an 11-year-old Haitian boy named Isaiah was diagnosed with cancer. He was such a spiritually sensitive child that I gave him the opportunity to preach one Sunday. Not knowing how long he would speak, I came prepared with my own message. However, he exceeded my expectations for duration and depth. For 45 minutes he taught from the book of Zechariah, which is filled with difficult passages.

But despite the congregation's hope-filled prayers for this gifted child to be healed, Isaiah died six months later. At his funeral, the church was packed to overflowing. When I played a five-minute audio recording of his sermon highlights, the impact was powerful. However, things didn't turn out as we had hoped for Isaiah. His death devastated his family, the community, and me personally. And yet hope endured. Isaiah's parents were eventually able to have another child. They named her Esther. Just as God used Queen Esther in the Bible account to bring new hope to his people after a period of darkness, so did the birth of this child bring new hope to Isaiah's parents and family.

Another couple at the church—Bert and Kim—had big plans for the future of their farm. However, Bert had to go through approximately 30 surgeries to repair his jaw. Kim shared with me that the "beginning of the end for Bert was when he was overradiated. From that point on he acquired every side effect you can think of. It was a real battle back and forth. We were discouraged and then hopeful." The couple went through many hardships and disappointments due to his health issues, and the church supported them through prayer and service. But, like Isaiah, Bert eventually died despite all of our fervent prayers. Kim, a fighter, still pursued their dream of starting a restaurant at the farm, but eventually she had to sell the business. Yet through this time, the Lord sustained Kim as she held on to the hope we have in Jesus Christ.

And then there was Rebecca, who recently shared her testimony on Facebook. Along with her story, she posted a picture of the day I baptized her. Here is her post:

> Every painful experience of my past prepared me for this day, and for a future purpose that has the potential to impact countless lives around me, prayerfully for the good. The setbacks I have endured since this day have only worked to strengthen me and to pave the way for God's purpose in my life to come to fruition. Even those challenging, gut-wrenching, want to give up times, are used to refine our character.
>
> In the six years since this day I was baptized, I have battled almost being homeless, getting my truck repossessed, and leaving a career that I made a lot of money in for one that I don't. I have lost friendships and have struggled to finally end an eating disorder that I have battled since I was a child. I have wailed and sobbed over things that haven't gone as I thought they would, should or even could have, but I have also been blessed to see the beauty, the glory, and the majesty of God.
>
> This life is like the tides of the very ocean I chose to be baptized in. When I made the decision to make the public declaration that Jesus Christ is my Lord and Savior, it would have been easy to have Ben Foley baptize me at the church. However, I wanted something more meaningful in regard to the personal battles that were to be buried when I went under the water.
>
> I chose Manasquan Beach, a place where my grandparents had a house just three blocks away, as well as the

place my Mom lived for a short while. Many, many days and nights were spent swimming, playing volleyball, walking the boardwalk, playing video games at Gee Gee's, and pondering life at the inlet. It was also the place of great heartache for me. A place that, at the time, added to my anger toward God. I was raped as a teenager in the home of a man who rented a house there. A place I should have never been.

An event that should have never happened . . . but it did. A tragic event, along with others prior, that God allowed in my life. Events that made me bitter and resentful. Events that, in most people's minds, a "loving God" would not and should not let happen . . . but he did.

It has taken me decades to heal from those events. And NONE of it could have happened without the healing that only Jesus can provide. No pills, therapy or hospital stays were able to break down the walls I had constructed around myself. No one has ever been able to get to the deepest parts of my broken heart like Jesus has.

The moment I said, "I give up," the very same God that I had hated for allowing such injustices to occur in my life, was the same one who showed up when I called. Despite my rage and blasphemy over the years, he didn't hesitate to come to my rescue. Bloody, handcuffed and hobbled into the back of a cop car, God revealed himself to me. A moment I cannot explain, nor do I think I will ever truly comprehend, but one that I am extremely grateful for. A moment that forever changed the trajectory of my life.

> It has taken me decades to heal from those events. And NONE of it could have happened without the healing that only Jesus can provide.

Jesus desires for us to call on him in our darkest moments. He desires for us to come to him when we realize that we have come to an end of ourselves and have no one else and nothing left. When we are at our weakest is when he comes and gives us his strength.[2]

As you can see from Rebecca's life, and the others from the church in New Jersey, she was not spared from some difficult situations. But her story, along with the others, is one of hope and redemption! It's a story of God's faithfulness and beauty arising from the ashes of her life.

Everything is against me!

Genesis chapter 46 tells the story of the patriarch Jacob who has received amazing promises from God. At this juncture in the narrative, he finds himself exasperated with how life is panning out, leading him to utter, "Everything is against me!"

I can relate to Jacob, and I'm guessing you can too, so let me tell you his story.

Because of a famine, the sons of Jacob are sent to Egypt to try to obtain food. However, their journey to Egypt sets in motion something much bigger than they realize. Years earlier, eleven of the sons of Jacob let jealousy overtake them, and they sold their brother Joseph to a caravan of traders, who sold him into slavery when they arrived in Egypt. For all they knew, that was the last they would see of him, and for all Joseph knew, that was the last he would ever see of his family (Genesis 37).

Years pass, and during that time Joseph undertakes quite a journey. First, he is the slave of a man named Potiphar, an official of Pharaoh, and captain of his guard. Joseph quickly gains Potiphar's trust and favor. However, he also gains the admiration of Potiphar's wife, who tries to seduce him. Joseph's refusal makes her so angry that she falsely accuses him of trying to rape her. This results in prison time for Joseph. But even there, the Lord is with Joseph, and he quickly gains the favor of the prison guard who puts him in charge of the other prisoners (Genesis 39:1-23).

One day two men—a baker and a cupbearer—are thrown into prison for offending Pharaoh. Each man has a dream that Joseph interprets. Joseph informs the baker that he will be put to death for his offense, but Pharaoh will let the cupbearer go and restore him to his position. Joseph pleads with the cupbearer to remember him and speak up on his behalf. However, Joseph's hopes are dashed once more because he hears nothing from the cupbearer. Joseph has been forgotten (Genesis 40:1-23).

The Lord is with Joseph.

Two years later, Pharaoh has two dreams. This situation shakes the cupbearer's memory so that he remembers Joseph. And so, Joseph is brought before Pharaoh to interpret the dreams. God gives Joseph the meaning of the dreams, which are about an approaching famine. As a result, Joseph's life has another sudden reversal: he is immediately appointed to be second in charge of all of Egypt, responsible for overseeing the storage and distribution of grain to prepare for seven years of famine.

It is during the famine that Joseph's brothers travel to Egypt looking for grain. When they came before Joseph, he immediately recognizes his brothers, even though they don't recognize him. There and then Joseph begins testing his brothers in a couple of ways to see how they will react. He wants to see if his brothers have experienced a change of heart or regret selling him into slavery. As part of that test, Joseph sends the brothers back to Israel with the request to bring their youngest brother, Benjamin, back with them, so they all will be together. In the meantime, Joseph keeps his brother Simeon with him as security.

Forgiveness found in Egypt

Put yourself in Jacob's shoes for a moment. All this time, he believes Joseph to be dead, because that's what his sons have told him. His son Simeon is now being kept in Egypt and will stay there until the other sons take Benjamin (his youngest) away from home and bring him to Egypt. Under these circumstances, and without the benefit of knowing how this story unfolds, you can sympathize with the exasperation of Jacob when he declares, *You have deprived me of my children. Joseph is no more, and Simeon is no more, and now you want to take Benjamin. Everything is against me!* (Genesis 42:36).

It certainly would appear that everything is against Jacob if you don't know the rest of the story. Have you, like Jacob, ever felt the same way? Maybe right now you are going through a season or situation where, judging by all appearances, everything is against you. And yet, things are not always what they appear to be. Appearances can be deceiving.

Suffice to say that Joseph reveals himself to his brothers, forgives them, and is reunited with his father. The whole family eventually comes to live with Joseph in Egypt, where all their needs are taken care of. In this way Joseph becomes a kind of "savior" to his own family for generations to come. The people of Israel are spared from death by famine. Joseph will later articulate the following to his brothers:

> *"You intended to harm me, but God intended it for good to accomplish what is now being done, the saving of many lives. So then, don't be afraid. I will provide for you and your children." And he reassured them and spoke kindly to them.* (Genesis 50:20-21)

What a powerful example of Joseph's forgiveness toward his brothers who had so deeply wounded him! God was not against Joseph, his brothers, or Jacob. God was, in fact, working on their behalf, even though the process was painful, and hope seemed to be lost! And eventually, Jesus Christ, the Messiah, would come from Jacob's family line. Things are not always what they appear to be.

Consider this wonderful biblical promise:

And we know that in all things God works for the good of those who love him, who have been called according to his purpose . . .

What, then, shall we say in response to these things? If God is for us, who can be against us? He who didn't spare his own Son, but gave him up for us all—how will he not also, along with him, graciously give us all things? Who will bring any charge against those whom God has chosen? It's God who justifies. Who then is the one who condemns? No one. Christ Jesus who died—more than that, who was raised to life—is at the right hand of God and is also interceding for us. Who shall separate us from the love of Christ? Shall trouble or hardship or persecution or famine or nakedness or danger or sword? As it is written:

> *"For your sake we face death all day long;*
> *we are considered as sheep to be slaughtered."*

No, in all these things we are more than conquerors through him who loved us. For I am convinced that neither death nor life, neither angels nor demons, neither the present nor the future, nor any powers, neither height nor depth, nor anything else in all creation, will be able to separate us from the love of God that is in Christ Jesus our Lord. (Romans 8:28, 31-39)

Forgiveness found in Ivory Coast

Recently I received this story from a woman named Adele who lives in Ivory Coast, Africa.

The Lord woke me up at night and asked me to read page twelve in *The Basic Things You Need to Know About Jesus* book from *ServeNow*. I woke up and opened my booklet on page twelve. The words were on forgiveness. To my surprise, my neighbor knocks on my door in the morning in tears. She told me that her husband has had affairs outside his home. Then I decided to go and meet her husband. He acknowledged this shameful act and said that he was ashamed of it and will never repeat it again. It was at this moment that I understood why the Lord made me read that exact text at night. So, I told him about God's forgiveness to all of us human beings who have disappointed him as our Creator. I explained to him that despite that, he sent his son Jesus to redeem us and give us life. I shared also that Jesus asks us to forgive all those who offend us. By God's grace, peace has returned to this home. And then, even greater news, shortly after, the husband received this forgiveness and gave his life to the Lord.

What an amazing story of redemption! Even in the worst situations, when our life story seems beyond hope, the God of all hope can show up and write a brand new chapter. He can bring something good out of our darkest moments.

We never know the full story in advance

The challenges we face are the constraints of time and our not knowing the full story in advance. We are not privy to all the details of what God is doing in the world or in our lives. We don't know the big picture of what he's preparing for the generations after us. God dwells *outside* of time, while operating *in* time. He sees the end from the beginning. He knows the full story and all the details along the way. In the meantime, he calls us to trust him even when things do not make sense and circumstances seem to be against us. He never promised the process would be easy or the road would be smooth. However, he has promised to be faithful and work all things together for good, even when what happens to us is not good and seems like hope is lost.

I received a heart-breaking story recently from a woman in Uganda who lost her son due to the lockdown measures implemented for COVID-19. She was sharing with us how meaningful a special booklet we wrote called *The Basic Things You Need to Know When Our World Falls Apart* was to her during this time. With tears in her eyes she explained to our national coordinator:

> This booklet has spearheaded my victory and freedom during my toughest times during this coronavirus/lockdown season. I lost my son during the first intense lockdown. He became seriously ill, yet no public or private transport was allowed unless permission was given from the Residential District Commissioner (RDC), who was miles away. Though I communicated to my relatives who could have given a hand with the medical bills, they were not able to travel due to the strong lockdown rules either. I tearfully watched my son breathe his last breath from home. This left me with many questions: "Isn't God a caring God?" "Why did he cause the sickness during this lockdown season?" At least I would have taken him to the hospital. With this and many more questions ringing in my mind, we were given the booklet about when our world falls apart. It was directly speaking to me. I was encouraged by the stories in the booklet, like the one about a lady who had gone to church but when she returned home she found her mother-in-law dead in the collapsed house due to an earthquake. This story encouraged me to trust God like this lady. I was encouraged and uplifted. Had it not been for the book, I would still be hopeless.

God seldom promises a smooth journey

One of the most intriguing stories in the New Testament is toward the end of the book of Acts. The apostle Paul is being taken away to Rome as a prisoner to stand trial. The Lord has told him that he will testify there on his behalf. But the Lord never tells him it will be a smooth journey getting there. In fact, notice the language used to describe their experience in Acts 27:4-20:

From there we put out to sea again and passed to the lee of Cyprus because the winds were against us. When we had sailed across the open sea off the coast of Cilicia and Pamphylia, we landed at Myra in Lycia. There the centurion found an Alexandrian ship sailing for Italy and put us on board. We made slow headway for many days and had difficulty arriving off Cnidus. When the wind did not allow us to hold our course, we sailed to the lee of Crete, opposite Salmone. We moved along the coast with difficulty and came to a place called Fair Havens, near the town of Lasea.

Much time had been lost, and sailing had already become dangerous because by now it was after the Day of Atonement. So Paul warned them, "Men, I can see that our voyage is going to be disastrous and bring great loss to ship and cargo, and to our own lives also." But the centurion, instead of listening to what Paul said, followed the advice of the pilot and of the owner of the ship. Since the harbor was unsuitable to winter in, the majority decided that we should sail on, hoping to reach Phoenix and winter there. This was a harbor in Crete, facing both southwest and northwest.

When a gentle south wind began to blow, they saw their opportunity; so they weighed anchor and sailed along the shore of Crete. Before very long, a wind of hurricane force, called the Northeaster, swept down from the island. The ship was caught by the storm and could not head into the wind; so we gave way to it and were driven along. As we passed to the lee of a small island called Cauda, we were hardly able to make the lifeboat secure, so the men hoisted it aboard. Then they passed ropes under the ship itself to hold it together. Because they were afraid they would run aground on the sandbars of Syrtis, they lowered the sea anchor and let the ship be driven along. We took such a violent battering from the storm that the next day they began to throw the cargo overboard. On the third day, they threw the ship's tackle overboard with their own hands. When neither sun nor stars appeared for many days and the storm continued raging, we finally gave up all hope of being saved.

Yikes! This isn't even the whole story. The ship is eventually shipwrecked, and their journey detoured further, but even though all hope seemed lost, they did eventually arrive at their intended destination. It reminds me of a classic picture that depicts life's journey visually in this way:[3]

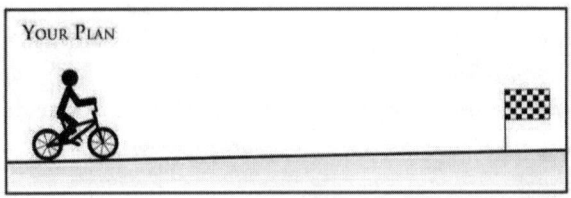

Often, the real problem for us has to do with our expectations and the conclusions we draw from our circumstances. We expect life to be smooth sailing, and so when it's not, we think God has abandoned us. We look at our circumstances and lose hope thinking everything is against us, because difficult things happen. We take God's promises but do not see the usual painful process of those promises unfolding in ways that sometimes seem contrary to what he has promised. So, when life takes its seemingly unfavorable twists and turns, we get confused, discouraged, and lose hope. As God's people, we often tend to emphasize his promises but fail to be honest about the process and pain that can be involved. That's why I wanted to share these stories from Scripture, because they highlight the fact that life is messy, yet God is faithful. God's path will not be a straight, smooth line. There will be setbacks, struggles, difficulties, and discouragements.

Even when I don't see it, you're working

We must face the fact that there are times in life that Jesus will not shy away from leading us into fierce storms that may threaten our lives. This is exactly what happened in Mark 4:35-41. The full story goes like this:

> That day when evening came, he said to his disciples, "Let us go over to the other side." Leaving the crowd behind, they took him along, just as he was, in the boat. There were also other boats with him. A furious squall came up, and the waves broke over the boat, so that it was nearly swamped. Jesus was in the stern, sleeping on a cushion. The disciples woke him and said to him, "Teacher, don't you care if we drown?" He got up, rebuked the wind and said to the waves, "Quiet! Be still!" Then the wind died down and it was completely calm. He said to his disciples, "Why are you so afraid? Do you still have no faith?" They were terrified and asked each other, "Who is this? Even the wind and the waves obey him!"

Did you notice a couple of important facts about this story? It was Jesus who came up with this travel idea. While Jesus was not the one who created the storm, he did allow his disciples to go through this storm. He was also with them the entire time through the storm. By appearances, it seemed to the disciples that Jesus didn't care. Suddenly they saw his power in the middle of this storm, and they came out on the other side in awe of Jesus, having experienced something that was only possible because of the storm. They no doubt experienced some damage to their boat and to their nerves, but they did survive this seemingly hopeless situation!

As Sinach, a Nigerian singer and songwriter, put it in a widely popular Christian worship song called "*Way Maker*":

> Even when I don't feel it, You're working
> You never stop, You never stop working

Everything may seem against you. But God is always for you! All hope may seem lost. But the God we serve is the God of all hope who makes a way even when there seems to be no way!

2

The God of All Hope

And now these three remain: faith, hope, and love.
—1 Corinthians 13:13

Approximately 2,000 years ago, the apostle Paul penned those words, and they're still quite well known and often quoted. In this one verse, Paul summed up the essence of the Christian faith and life. In just three words, he boiled down basic Christianity to its most essential ingredients. Those three irreplaceable dynamics are faith, hope, and love. Today we hear quite a lot about faith and especially love, but we don't hear as much about the word sandwiched in the middle. And yet, it may be what people in the world need the most: real and lasting hope.

Hope is not wishful thinking

If hope is not wishful thinking, what is it? Why is it so important? Where can we find it? How do we sustain it?

Let us start with what biblical hope is *not*. The kind of hope that the apostle Paul was referring to in 1 Corinthians 13:13 isn't a wishy-washy kind of superstitious luck. It's not the kind of uncertain hope when we say things like, "I hope my favorite team wins the championship this year." It's not the kind of hope where we hope "bad things" won't happen to us, or that we'll be spared trouble or hardship. It's not a hope that denies reality or is escapism from the harsher realities of life. It's not a hope that is pure optimism or "positive thinking."

Hope originates from God

The kind of hope the Bible speaks of is confident and sure. Hope is rooted in God's character and nature, despite our feelings or situations. It's a hope anchored in not just God's promises but in his very person. It's a hope that is eternal in nature and provides confidence found not in ourselves or in our circumstances. It's a hope rooted in Jesus and what he has accomplished on our behalf by his grace and great love for us. It's not a hope that looks inward or tries harder to pull ourselves together in our own resources. Rather, it looks upward and draws upon a supernatural yet real strength.

Hebrews 6:17-20 states,

> *Because God wanted to make the unchanging nature of his purpose very clear to the heirs of what was promised, he confirmed it with an oath. God did this so that, by two unchangeable things in which it is impossible for God to lie, we who have fled to take hold of the hope set before us may be greatly encouraged. We have this hope as an anchor for the soul, firm and secure. It enters the inner sanctuary behind the curtain, where our forerunner, Jesus, has entered on our behalf. He has become a high priest forever.*

The kind of hope we want you to find within this book is a hope that originates from God, is extended to us by God, and results in our being greatly encouraged in God. He is a God who provides security, stability, and a solid foundation in the face of any and all vicious storms we endure in this life. This kind of hope will help us weather all emotional turmoil and earthly distress. It gives us a resolve we cannot muster in our own strength. It's a kind of hope that tethers our lives here on earth with the reality of heaven in a way that allows us to face tomorrow, no matter what we may be going through today.

This kind of hope gives us the endurance we need in what I like to call the "in-between," the place in between the promises of God and the fulfillment of those promises. In more cases than not, that is the place we find ourselves for the longest periods of time and therefore need the most encouragement.

Hope casts all things in a new light

In his book *All Things New*, John Eldredge writes,

> Hope is the sunlight of the soul; without it, our inner world walks about in shadows. But like a sunrise in the heart, hope sheds light over our view of everything else, casting all things in a new light.[1]

Our prayer is that through this book, you will find needed encouragement. We are praying that hope will arise deep within your being for your own life and that you will encounter the God of all hope in a new and fresh way for the challenges **Hope is the sunlight of the soul.** of today's world. There is a great prayer in Romans 15:13 that expresses it in this way: *May the God of hope fill you with all joy and peace as you trust in him, so that you may overflow with hope by the power of the Holy Spirit.* This prayer reminds us that hope is not just something God gives. Hope is who he is—the God of hope!

An elderly woman in Uganda shared the following testimony with us after she read *The Basic Things You Need to Know About the Holy Spirit.*

> One day I was stressed by many things in my life, and tears kept flowing. Early in the morning, after a sleepless night, I started reading *The Basic Series* booklet about the Holy Spirit. As I was reading, I came across the comment about the Holy

Spirit being a comforter! At that moment, I felt someone comforting me, and my pain and troubles disappeared. I am grateful for this booklet and for the work the Holy Spirit has done and is still doing in my life.

Hope through the Holy Spirit

We know we are experiencing the God of hope when we find ourselves being filled and even overflowing with joy and peace. If that seems impossible to you, take heart! This kind of hope is something that can happen only by the power of the Holy Spirit. It is not something we can work up or work ourselves into. It is a gift from God as you trust in him. In other words, it is God's responsibility to impart hope to our hearts in a way that fills us to overflowing with joy and peace. Our responsibility is to trust in him.

Pretend you are a jar that is empty with a lid on top. When the cover is on top of the jar, nothing can get in, and nothing can get out. However, when the lid comes off or is even opened slightly, some other substance other than air can enter. Also, it's now possible for whatever is in the jar to come out. When we trust in God, we are opening the lid so that he can pour hope into us, so that we not only experience joy and peace, but when others encounter us, they can also benefit from the overflow!

I really want to encourage you and myself as well. By nature and personality, I am prone to discouragement and even depression at times. I can easily imagine the worst in any given situation. In fact, I am often driven by fear of what could go wrong or what might not happen! I have my moments of mustering great optimism and faith. Still, much more of the time, I am naturally pessimistic. After a season of being up, I tend to gravitate back down.

Maybe you are by nature different from me. Perhaps you are more an optimist who sees the good in situations and looks on the bright side. As a result, you may think this book is not as much for you as it may be for someone like me, but let me challenge you. There is a difference between looking on the bright side and the kind of hope imparted to us by God. This kind of hope is something beyond personality and temperament. It's something that can be received only from the God of all hope. And regardless of whether you are pessimistic or optimistic or somewhere in between, we

> There is a difference between looking on the bright side and the kind of hope imparted to us by God.

all have seasons or situations in our lives that require something beyond what we can muster through our own efforts or strengths.

Do not be afraid

Did you know the most often repeated command in Scripture outside of "Praise the Lord" is along the lines of "Do not be afraid" or "Do not be discouraged" or "Take courage" and "Be of good cheer"? There is a reason for this! God knows, no matter who we are, that we face situations where fear grips our hearts and despair sets in, and so we need this reminder.

Even the strongest believers or most faithful servants of God need fresh hope. For example, at *ServeNow* we love to give bicycles to pastors who have no other means of transportation. So much is our enthusiasm, our partner in Uganda has a dream to provide 10,000 bicycles to pastors in his country alone! One pastor, who was full of joy after receiving a bicycle, told us, "I have been walking 34 miles daily, and I was about to give up. But now I feel the freshness in me as if my journey in ministry has started today, forgetting the last ten years of struggle. I am so grateful for today."

Another pastor in Asia explained his joy this way:

> Until yesterday, I have been walking 16 miles every day to reach my mission field, and the extreme summer heat has

been taking a toll on my health. Last week, as I walked to conduct a Sunday service, I felt faint and almost collapsed due to the heat and profuse perspiration. The very next day, I received a call from *ServeNow* about the gift of a bicycle for me and other pastors and evangelists like me. This gift has changed my life and equipped me to work more efficiently to expand God's kingdom. It has reaffirmed my faith in the Lord who I serve, that he always looks out for his own! In the 20-some years that I have been working as an evangelist, planting churches in the unreached regions of the Dooars [India], this is the first time anyone has asked about the well-being of the pastors and missionaries. Everyone is focused on how well or bad the response from the believers is or how much growth we are seeing in the Church—which is good. Still, nobody had ever wanted to talk about the hardships missionaries and pastors face. When *ServeNow* approached me and asked me how I travel to places, and if a bicycle would help, it was my prayer coming true. Thank you, *ServeNow*, for your heart to care for us!

Whether you are a committed Christian, a faithful servant, a new believer, a person stagnant in your walk with God, or someone who doesn't yet know God, I am praying that you presently will experience the God of all hope, through the pages of this book.

Hope rising against all possible hope

There is a messy but beautiful story in Genesis 16. Abraham and his wife Sarah have been given a hope-filled promise about having many descendants. As the years go by, they become older and older, and the odds of producing a child diminish. In desperation, they decide to take matters into their own hands, and Abraham sleeps with their servant Hagar. She gives birth to a son, but it's not the son that God has promised Abraham and Sarah.

Additionally, this relationship results in Sarah's jealousy, tension, and mistreatment of Hagar to such extent that she decides to run away. But while in the desert, the angel of the Lord finds Hagar near a spring in the desert, and he says, *Hagar, slave of Sarai, where have you come from, and where are you going?* (Genesis 16:7-8). Hagar goes on to explain her situation. In response, the angel of the Lord ministers to her in her unique situation and speaks blessing and promise over her. Here's what the Bible says is her response: *She gave this name to the LORD who spoke to her: 'You are the God who sees me,' for she said, 'I have now seen the One who sees me'* (Genesis 16:13).

Here's the point: The God of all hope sees you whatever your situation may be. No matter your challenges. No matter the circumstances. No matter what you are running away from. No matter the mess you are in. He is the One who sees you and desires to impart hope into your life.

Pastor Sognigbe from Benin, Africa shared with us the following testimony after he received and read the *Basic Series* booklet *The Basic Things You Need to Know When Our World Falls Apart*. He writes:

> Frankly, without exaggeration, this book is as if God came down from heaven to talk to me personally. Others, with whom I shared the booklet, had the same reaction! They all tell me how happy they are because the words in the book speak directly to difficulties and hardships they are passing through. Each section and each story illustrated in the book addresses something in our lives!

> He is the God who sees. He is the God of all hope.

3

As the World Gets Better, People Are Losing Hope

As Pharaoh approached, the Israelites looked up, and there were the Egyptians, marching after them. They were terrified and cried out to the LORD. They said to Moses, "Was it because there were no graves in Egypt that you brought us to the desert to die? What have you done to us by bringing us out of Egypt? Didn't we say to you in Egypt, 'Leave us alone; let us serve the Egyptians'? It would have been better for us to serve the Egyptians than to die in the desert!"

Moses answered the people, "Do not be afraid. Stand firm and you will see the deliverance the LORD will bring you today. The Egyptians you see today you will never see again. The LORD will fight for you; you need only to be still."
—Exodus 14:10-14

When was the last time you felt totally hopeless? Can you think of the last situation where you felt despair? Maybe you feel that way right now in some area of your life or about life in general. If so, you are not alone! Not to downplay anyone's individual circumstances, but there are many times in our lives where we get that sickening feeling deep in our stomachs and lose heart. Like the Israelites in the passage above, we "look up" and are terrified about our future or present situation. We even become irrational in our thoughts and lash out in anger at those closest to us and hurl accusations as we look to lay blame or find fault with someone else's decisions—even if we went along with it and agreed to it! We cave in to fear, and like a cornered animal, we fight back with whoever is nearby!

There is no doubt that as we look at the world today, there is much that can put fear in our hearts and cause us to lose hope. Just to name a few:

- According to UNHCR, the UN Refugee Agency, there were 79.5 million people displaced worldwide at the end of 2019. This is a record-high number of displaced people and refugees.[1]

- More than one billion people do not have a complete Bible in their language. Over 250 million people have no Bible in their language.[2]

- More Christians have been martyred in the 20th century than all other centuries combined. That number is only growing worldwide.[3]

- Natural disasters seem to come one after another somewhere in the world.[4]

- Diseases and illnesses kill millions of people every year.[5]

- Human trafficking is the fastest growing criminal industry in the world.[6]

- International and domestic terrorism is an ongoing threat and reality in the world.[7]

- Racial tensions, wars, and threats of nuclear war continue to rage and flare up worldwide.[8]

This list could go on with other real or perceived fears so many of us live with daily. While this may seem completely overwhelming, others have noted and argued that the world is, in fact, not getting worse but may be better, healthier, more prosperous, and safer than any other time in human history.

In the book *Factfulness*, the author Hans Rosling reveals a couple of realities that might surprise you. For example, he notes, "In the last 20 years, the proportion of the world population living in extreme poverty has almost halved."[9] Or what do you think about this question? "How many people in the world have some form of electricity?" The answer is 80 percent.[10]

Mark Manson, a secular author who makes an interesting case for the need for hope today, noted:

> People are more educated and literate than ever before. Violence has trended down for decades, possibly centuries. Racism, sexism, discrimination, and violence against women are at their lowest point in recorded history. We have more rights than ever before. Half the planet has access to the internet. Extreme poverty is at an all-time low worldwide. Wars are smaller and less frequent than at any other time in recorded history. Children are dying less, and people are living longer. There is more wealth than ever before. We've like, cured a bunch of diseases and stuff.[11]

Fareed Zakaria, in his book *The Post-American World*, also notes, "But don't believe everything you see on television. Our anecdotal impression turns out to be wrong. War and organized violence have declined dramatically over the last two decades." He goes on to quote Steven Pinker who "argues that today we are probably in the most peaceful time in our species existence." As Zakaria further explains, "The immediacy of the images and the intensity of the 24-hour news cycle combine to produce constant hyperbole. . . . It *feels* like a dangerous world. But it isn't."[12]

This does not diminish the horror of the realities listed in the beginning of this chapter or the fact that many people still live in extreme poverty. I am writing this book in the year 2020 when COVID-19 has pushed back progress on many of these levels. Acute hunger has been projected to double, for example, adding an additional 130 million more people facing starvation.[13] Children are going without education and back into child-labor type situations.[14] Human trafficking has not slowed down but increased during this time as the vulnerable are preyed upon.[15] Millions are being thrust into poverty.[16]

Despite that reality, it's still true to point out that the power of 24/7 news and social media in this digital age are making the world seem worse than it is. As John Eldredge writes in his book *Get Your Life Back*:

> While we've always had our individual struggles and heartbreaks to deal with, now we have the tragedies of the entire world delivered to us hourly on our mobile devices. This is all very hard on the soul. Traumatizing, in fact. Exposure to traumatic events can traumatize us, and we're getting lots of it in our feed. It's like we've been swept into the gravitational field of a digital black hole, which is sucking our lives from us.[17]

The problem is not material but spiritual

The real problem is not material but spiritual. John Eldredge describes this issue in another book, *All Things New*:

> Though we are trying to put a bold face on things, the human race is not doing well at all. Take any of our vital signs—you'll see. The rate of antidepressant use has gone through the ceiling in the last 20 years; antidepressants have become the third most common prescription drug . . . suicide rates are also skyrocketing; depending on the country, it is the first or

> **We've been swept into the gravitational living field of a digital black hole, which is sucking our lives from us.**

second leading cause of death among our young people . . . we appear to be suffering a great crisis of hope.[18]

Mark Manson further notes in his book on hope,

> We live in an interesting time in that, materially, things are arguably better than they have ever been before, yet we all seem to be losing our minds thinking the world is one giant toilet bowl about to be flushed. An irrational sense of hopelessness is spreading across the rich, developed world. It's a paradox of progress: the better things get, the more anxious and desperate we all seem to feel.[19]

Losing hope in the crises

So, what is going on? What is going on is a crisis and loss of hope. Mark Manson also offers these words:

> Our psyche needs hope to survive the way a fish needs water. Hope is the fuel for our mental engine . . . the opposite of happiness is hopelessness, an endless gray horizon of resignation and indifference. . . . Hopelessness is the root of anxiety, mental illness, and depression. It is the source of all misery and the cause of all addiction.[20]

These are strong words from a secular writer, recognizing a crisis of hope in our world and the overwhelming need for hope!

What we're really facing is a loss of hope in the goodness of God. This loss is a virus that has affected humanity since the fall in the Garden of Eden. It's one of the oldest lies of the enemy. The devil's focused

Our psyche needs hope to survive the way a fish needs water.

scheme described in Genesis 3 causes Adam and Eve to mistrust and doubt the goodness of God. By questioning what God really said as well as questioning his motives, the devil succeeds in getting Adam and Eve to doubt God's character and goodness. He is still effectively using this same scheme in our world today, causing people to lose hope in God and his goodness. This is what lies at the root of why this world is both fallen and broken. We have lost hope in a good God.

"What is truth?" or "What is good?"

Social commentators have noted a shift in the way that those labeled as Gen Z (those 25 and younger) approach the world. Their question is not so much "What is truth?" as some generations before, but "What is good?" For them, objective truth is not their reference point, but a more subjective anchor asking "Do I want to be like you?" They are wondering if there is a better way than what they have seen modeled.[21]

Older generations tend to shake their heads when I share this, as if to say "Yep, that's the problem in our world, truth no longer matters!" While I understand the sentiment and believe biblical truth is vital, I think answering Gen Z's question is an opportunity for us if we can adjust our approach to address what matters most to the next generation.

In Matthew 5:14-16 Jesus understood what was missing and explained it in this way:

> *You are the light of the world. A town built on a hill cannot be hidden. Neither do people light a lamp and put it under a bowl. Instead they put it on its stand, and it gives light to everyone in the house. In the same way, let your light shine before others, that they may see your good deeds and glorify your Father in heaven.*

Young people today are asking "What is good?" Therefore our "good works" versus "absolute truth statements" should draw them to see the goodness of God more easily and put their trust in him! Youth of today want their lives to matter. They are into causes, movements, and impact. They want to be engaged. They want to make a difference. And words are not enough! They need to see the Gospel in action through good deeds. They are rightly tired of our words not matching our actions. They see one scandal after another unfolding among prominent and once celebrated evangelical leaders. They smell hypocrisy a mile away. Jim Cymbala writes in his book *Storm,*

> Surveys also show that there is barely any difference between the lifestyles of Christian churchgoers and the behavior of those who don't believe in God at all. Yet the Scriptures define believers in Jesus as "saints," a people who have been separated from the world and belong exclusively to Jesus.[22]

Lessons from Uganda

Over the years *ServeNow's* partner in Uganda realized that words can only go so far. In his country, many were preaching the Gospel but not living the Gospel. It was leaving a bad taste in people's mouths. They would say things, like "God bless you" but not respond to people's needs. However, when this Ugandan leader began focusing on meeting people's needs, he found that his words, and the Good News of the Gospel, truly became good news and changed people's lives. That is why he now likes to say, "the Gospel of deeds supersedes the Gospel of words." Yes, the Gospel is a declaration of Good News, but if it's only words to people in need, then how can it truly be good news? Jesus didn't just go around preaching and teaching. He also went around healing people,

The Gospel of deeds supersedes the Gospel of words.

delivering people, serving people, and meeting needs. The apostle Peter once put it this way in Acts 10:37-38:

> *You know what has happened throughout the province of Judea, beginning in Galilee after the baptism that John*

preached—how God anointed Jesus of Nazareth with the Holy
Spirit and power, and how he went around doing good and
healing all who were under the power of the devil, because God
was with him.

Jesus backed up his words with his actions, and thus his words
had power!

Over the years, people have often asked us why *ServeNow* isn't
single-minded. Why don't we just preach the Gospel? Why don't
we just give out Bibles? Why don't we simply focus on human
trafficking? Because of this American business mindset, some
struggle to understand what *ServeNow* does.

Following the Jesus model

But in reality it's very simple, and it follows the same model as Jesus did. I like to tell people that Jesus came for one main purpose,
but he didn't do just one thing! In fact, I absolutely love how the
Gospel of John concludes. John noted, *Jesus did many other things*
as well. If every one of them were written down, I suppose that even
the whole world would not have room for the books that would be
written (John 21:25). And that was in just three and a half years!
Imagine all that Jesus has done since then over the past 2,000
years and is still doing today through his people around the world!

I am always amazed at the impact *ServeNow* has had during
its first few years. For example, in our first seven years we served in
some specific, measurable, and direct ways more than 3.5 million
people worldwide. More than 800,000 copies of *The Basic Series*
booklets have been placed in as many sets of hands in multiple
languages. Over 1,500 vulnerable women have participated in
skill-training programs to prevent human trafficking or prostitution and have viewed these programs as their only "hope."

It hasn't been just one thing but many things. The greatest
needs that will make the greatest impact are different in different

communities and countries at different times. But the result is the same. Over and over again, people's lives have been transformed, and they discover the God of all hope.

I will never forget a Hindu woman whose village had just suffered terrible flooding. The problem was not just floods destroying homes, but the water was also threatening people's lives. Elderly people and children were especially vulnerable. The *ServeNow* staff decided to send a team to this devastated area to conduct medical clinics. When this suffering family was treated, the mother shared the following testimony, "I was growing worried for my ten children as people were falling sick. So, I began to pray to all my gods. But it appears your God has heard and answered our prayers!"

Do you know what I hear when I listen to these kinds of testimonies? I hear the words of Jesus: *Let your light shine before others,*

> **It appears your God has heard and answered our prayers!**

that they may see your good deeds and glorify your Father in heaven (Matthew 5:16). Good deeds reveal a good God!

Does your God have power?

In much of the Western World the more common questions about God have been, "What is truth and what are your beliefs?" But in the Eastern world the question is quite different. It goes like this, "Does your God have power?" Additionally, in the Western World, we are very materialistic. For us, a physical object is just a physical object. But that is not the case in other parts of the world such as Asia and Africa. In those regions, a physical object is symbolic and represents a message. That is why *ServeNow* continually receives testimonies that explains the value of the physical object used to assist in a difficult situation. For example, after wrapping blankets around some people in an area where temperatures were close to freezing, I remember one woman specifically saying, "I experienced God's love through this blanket you gave to me and my child." Good deeds reveal a good God! Acts done in love open hearts and doors for the Gospel!

Early on in *ServeNow's* short history, we received a testimony from a pastor who had been ministering in his village for 20 years. It was a predominantly Muslim community where the people were hostile toward him. The pastor shared that the people would "spit on my shadow when I walked by, to show their disgust toward me." However, when *ServeNow* partnered with the pastor to provide a free medical clinic in his community, the results were astonishing. Through this simple action people later commented that the medicine that was provided was powerful but his prayers for them were even more powerful! Because of that deed, they began opening up their homes to him and asked him to come by for tea and to pray for other relatives and needs. Others began coming to his church to hear God's word, and his church began to grow.

Even some of the more aggressive Muslim areas in the world are catching on to the power of deeds. In parts of Uganda for example, Muslims are copying what Christians have historically done in providing education, food, and health services. As they tap into universal needs, they are growing their numbers significantly. It's sad that in many Christian circles we have lost our passion for good works or completely separated them from the proclamation of the Gospel. Jesus has called us to both the Great Commission, which means to go and make disciples of all nations and the Great Commandment, which includes to love God and love your neighbor as yourself. At *ServeNow* we like to say we come with a cup of cold water in one hand and a Bible in the other. It doesn't need to be an either-or. It can be both-and!

In many parts of Asia, children have never had an opportunity to attend a summer camp or a Vacation Bible School program. Sunita was one of the children who attended a *ServeNow* Vacation Bible School camp in one of the city slums in South Asia. Even though she comes from a Hindu family, Sunita had recently started attending Sunday school regularly. Here is her story in her own words:

> Ever since I started to attend school, I was made to believe I am different than others because of my skin condition. There are not many children who want to be friends with me and that makes me sad. What I enjoyed the most about being at this camp were the lessons on how God loves each one of us, in spite of our differences.

Transformational change in young people

We noticed a similar reality in *ServeNow's* summer-camp programs in Ukraine. Just as in Asia, 80 percent of the children who attend our camps are not coming from a Christian background, church, or have any knowledge of God's love for them. But a high percentage of them leave the camp after just 10 days not only having had the time of their life but also with Christ in their hearts and God's love as a reality in their lives.

One young girl, whose name is Liza, shared the following after she had concluded the camp. "This is my first time being around Christians. I did not know God is good!" When she came home, she started taking a bus by herself to a church in the next town, which happens to be the church where our Ukrainian National Directors attend. After a couple of weeks she asked if she could sing a worship song during the service. (I was sent a video and I have to say it was one of the most delightful videos I have ever watched.) Her mom even came that Sunday and has continued attending Sunday after Sunday. The following year, I had the opportunity to preach at this Ukrainian church, and that Sunday, Liza sang with a radiant joy I have rarely seen. After the service, the church was having a charity picnic to raise money for train tickets for children to be able to go to summer camp. It was so touching to observe Liza and another camp friend sitting at a table where they sold their own items and pictures to help other children attend camp!

Signs of his goodness

Let me return to the goodness of God once more, even in the face of circumstances that might seem to undermine it. In our short history as a mission organization and being a part of a larger worldwide movement, we've had many challenging months when we sometimes didn't know how we were going to make it financially or where funding would come from for certain projects. However, we have repeatedly watched God faithfully take care of us, meet our needs, and surprise us with what our finance director and I like to refer to as "signs of his goodness."

I share this because it has everything to do with hope. Sometimes we do not have all the answers or solutions. But I encourage you to look for "signs of the goodness of God." Stay focused on God's goodness. Ask God to give you "signs of his goodness" to restore your hope. Did you know that is a biblical prayer? For example, it's prayed in Psalm 86:17, *Give me a sign of your goodness, that my enemies may see it and be put to shame, for you, LORD, have helped me and comforted me.* And let us remember the words of Psalm 34:8, *Taste and see that the LORD is good; blessed is the one who takes refuge in him.*

Here is one final testimony from the world of *ServeNow* to encourage you today. Our team in India went to provide blankets to people in a village in the Himalayan mountains who face freezing temperatures inside their homes because there are no heat sources. The blankets the team handed out were something more than a blanket to these people! The village chief in this region verbalized it this way, "This quality blanket means hope to survive the winter. Before, I had only heard that Christians do such social service, but this is the first time I encountered such an act of love. I am excited to know about the Gospel message and the truth about salvation in Christ. Your God is a loving God!"

At the beginning of this chapter we showed that despite all the challenges that still exist, the world is improving. But at the same time, people may need more than ever to experience the hope found in the goodness of God. That hope is made real through our actions. Good deeds reveal a good God. Keep tasting of the goodness of God and keep showing others the goodness of God!

4

Hope Began with a Toilet

Hope deferred makes the heart sick,
but a longing fulfilled is a tree of life.
—Proverbs 13:12

In the summer of 2012, I (Lars) retired as president of a not-for-profit organization after founding it 14 years earlier. At that point I was rather burned out, and in my unrealistic simplicity, I thought it would be possible for me to remain working in some other staff position in the organization that had cost me sweat, tears, and some major financial involvement. But it also gave me no end of joy, as it had grown from one small project to serving countries with a dedicated global staff at its peak of more than 120 internationals.

After the tsunami of 2004, which hit India, Sri Lanka, Thailand, and Indonesia, we provided a massive assistance program to thousands of people who had lost everything by providing "buckets of love," which were filled with useful items. In 2005 after hurricane Katrina hit the United States, we did the same. Using a 10-month training program, we equipped some 5,000 ministers in India, Nepal, Honduras, El Salvador, and Ukraine. Through these years I also had an opportunity to address more than 50,000 pastors on almost all continents, representing many more denominations than I knew existed.

Suddenly it was over, and for months I sat at home in my basement office staring at the wall. Was life over just because I had turned 68 and the organization needed younger leadership? My hands, legs, heart, and brain were still willing to undertake expressions of the Great Commission, but there seemed to be no way forward. I lost all hope and sank into a deep depression, with sadness, hurt, and even anger.

In my depressed state, I tried to read and study the Scriptures. One morning a verse jumped out at me. I had probably read it more than 100 times before in my life, but now it spoke to me as if it were delivered through a megaphone. The words of the prophet Joel became alive to me. *Then, after doing all those things, I will pour out my Spirit upon all people. Your sons and daughters will prophesy. Your old men will dream dreams, and your young men will see visions* (Joel 2:28, NLT). Wow! Indeed I was old, at least in other people's eyes! But I could still dream new dreams!

For weeks I mulled this verse over, not sure what the Lord had in mind. I did know that there were still enormous needs around the world as far as sharing the Gospel was concerned. But how could I do anything about it?

ServeNow *is born*

A few weeks later, my wife Doreen and I were invited to Houston by our close friends Mike and Cynthia Richards. They wanted to celebrate the 50 years Doreen and I had spent in ministry. For more than 30 years, we had spent time together in a variety of ministries focused on spreading the Word of God around the world. Mike and Cynthia invited some of their close friends, whom we also knew, to a private dinner at a restaurant. What a night that would become! After presenting me with a certificate from the then governor of Texas, Rick Perry, making me an honorary Texas citizen, I was also presented a set of gorgeous Texas boots, with the implied message, "It's not over; you need to die with your boots on!"

One of the guests asked me, "So what are you going to do in the next few years?" Not quite knowing how to answer, I simply blurted out, "Well, I may be writing a few books in the future." Little did I know that over the next eight years I would write or edit more than 30 booklets for *ServeNow*, which have been used globally by more than 800,000 people so far!

Through the late hours of the evening into the early hours of the morning, my host and I sat by his living room fireplace and brainstormed. Without his knowing, some of his words became a prophetic voice in my life: "You know, Lars, there are so many blind spots on the mission map, and you are one of the few that happen to be aware of them. What are you going to do about that? If you start anything up again, I will give you the first gift!"

On the plane on the way home the next day, Doreen and I discussed the events of the previous evening, and I shared what I sensed I had heard from God during Mike's and my discussions. She was somewhat negative to our getting involved in anything new, knowing the toll it had taken on both of us through the various organizations I had worked with as a leader for the past 50 years. Doreen had also been a lone parent with three children to raise while I traveled around the world fulfilling the ministry he had placed in my hands.

We had barely come home when our daughter Maria turned up. Without much conversation, she blurted, "Whatever the Lord is telling you to do, Andy [her husband] and I are 100 percent behind it!" I looked intently at her, and

> **"Whatever the Lord is telling you to do, Andy and I are 100 percent behind it!"**

responded with a smile, "You wouldn't like to be the executive director of a new mission organization, would you? If you do, I can probably serve as the chair of the board and train you." Maria, first alone, and then with her husband had spent many years with Youth With A Mission, serving with their teams all over Europe and Brazil, as well as in India on many occasions. Maria has such a heart for mission and understands how to work with nationals with culture differences, using imagination in moving forward as well as going to work with only a dollar or so in her pocket.

That day was really the birth of *ServeNow*! I had toyed with the word Serve in my mind for quite a while. Seeing I could die any moment, the word Now seemed appropriate to be added, so *ServeNow* was named that day. My son-in-law Andy came up with the tag line "Procrastinate later," which many people seem to muse about and remember.

Within three weeks we had pulled a board together, consulted a lawyer about incorporation, and drawn up the application for not-for-profit status, including IRS permission to become a tax-exempt 501(c)(3) organization. The application was filed New Year's Eve 2012, and then lo and behold, the IRS permission was granted in March 2013, not even three months after the application.

Hope began with a toilet

During the first weeks of 2013 we were a bit lost. We had no projects, no money, no donors except one, no staff, and not much hope we would survive our fast and early birth.

In early February 2013, I received an e-mail from a friend in Uganda, Rev. Moses Ssemanda Mbuga. I had met Moses under some strange circumstances a few years earlier. Sometime in 2011, I received a call from one of our partners in Florida. She excitedly told me that she had just heard about an outstanding man from Uganda, whom I absolutely had to meet. My initial response was "No, I don't!" Over the years I had met so many people from around the world who came to see me just to sell me on their project and wanting an immediate gift. She immediately responded, "No, you don't need to come here to see him. We will fly him to you if you only give him an hour of your time." That made it different, and I agreed. Moses came and we spent several *days* together.

During that time I heard a story of absolute hopelessness as well as stories of how hope had provided for thousands of people. Moses' father had been imprisoned under the evil president Idi Amin and tortured for his faith. After he was released, he continued to share the Gospel, and several churches were formed from his main church. When Moses was 25 years old, his father died after having been in a car accident. He pleaded with Moses to take care of his mother, siblings, and his church. Moses had 13 siblings, so he suddenly was feeding 15 mouths. He considered adding some orphans, and soon he had three more to feed. Moses continued:

> It seemed like I was not ready for it, and I needed help. The church my father pastored had grown to about 300 members, but after his death, the numbers started to fall, with members leaving because they believed I was too young to lead at the time. I was left with only 15 congregants and was ready to give up all hope! I was passionate to see people's lives transformed, but my journey was unclear, especially at such a young age. Faced with such challenges, I was torn between wanting to quit, and desperately wanting to continue serving. On the other hand, I did all kinds of odd jobs, trying to take care of my mother and siblings while continuing with the missionary work out in the rural areas. I worked with poor communities needing support and love, but at this time all the support was gone, and I was left by myself to figure out how I was going to continue serving these areas. My vision

was clear. Something deep within would not let me give up. It was at that time that I started having recurring dreams of orphans in our country. Our nation was just recovering from a period of war so at first, I didn't care about the dreams, thinking that the effects of war were weighing heavy on my mind. But the more dreams I had, the more attention I paid to them, asking myself why they kept coming back. Maybe I needed to do something, after all. However, I didn't want to start anything new at the time due to the challenges facing me, as well as the lack of resources to support the orphans.

In 1989, a friend of mine, with whom I shared my story, gave me a book which would later be my inspiration—the biography of George Müller. George Müller was a Christian evangelist and Director of the Ashley Down orphanage in Bristol, England, who has recorded that he cared for 10,024 orphans in his life. He was well known for providing education to the children under his care, to the point where he was accused of raising the poor above their natural station in life. Being a poor man himself, he didn't have the resources required to support them, but when asked how he was able to help them, he stated that he relied on his voice as an evangelist to raise awareness about them, and his faith in Christ. This is what I needed in such a difficult time.

At this point, I knew I had to do something. I had already witnessed astonishing levels of poverty within the communities I had served. Though I grew up in a poor home myself, the missionary work had exposed me to life and human suffering I'd thought unimaginable. The most affected were the children. There were no schools so children stayed home doing all sorts of jobs; what many of us would consider child labor. Young girls were forced into marriages with older men.

I also learned that many of these experiences existed in other parts of Uganda but were being addressed by some groups, partly because these areas were more accessible compared to the communities I worked with. We often used boats to sail through thick swamps to access areas. The roads were so poor and dangerous. There were also growing fears of people being ambushed by robbers while traveling to these communities. It would have been understandably difficult for anyone to reach out there.

I fell in love with these communities—places with no public electricity, healthcare, clean running water, yet the people had the warmest and brightest spirits and energy, like no worries existed in their lives. Over the next few months, I met children who taught me the meaning of courage, love, and perseverance. Many of them had suffered from diseases for years and yet kept pressing on, praying, hoping and surviving. It changed my life. I had to take a step of faith.

After starting with the three orphans in 1989, we now serve 3,000 children, educating and developing them, equipping them with skills to become productive leaders. We believed and stepped out in faith, and God has been faithful. I was blessed to have had a growing local team of compassionate individuals wanting to change the story of their land. That's why we couldn't wait for external funding to start—we used what we had; mud and sticks which we used to start our first schools yet seeing hundreds of children signing up to receive education for the first time. Little did we know this would help spring up eight learning centers across Uganda. Additionally, the persistence and faith in God enabled our church to grow as well to over 800 members, and 300 churches planted across Uganda and beyond to further the Gospel of our Lord.

I listened in amazement to a story of hope. He was not asking me for anything but wanted me to be aware of what they were doing. The story sounded too good to be true! To ensure it was for real, a friend of mine, Kyle Pewitt, who at that time was the mission pastor at Council Road Baptist Church in Bethany, Oklahoma, was going on a trip to Africa that included Uganda. I asked him to meet with Moses and then verify that what Moses had told me was for real. Kyle returned with hundreds of photos and videos and confirmed that it was very good and very true.

Now, several years later, I received an e-mail from Moses. He explained that a toilet building at one of his eight country schools had just imploded. None of the children were hurt, but they were in dire needs to replace the toilet building as soon as possible. Could I somehow help? Moses didn't know anything about our new venture, but this was an answer from God.

I called Maria and asked her, "Can we start a ministry with a toilet?" She told me to test it. So, I sent an e-mail to some 150 friends whom I knew well, to see if anyone would respond. Overnight I went from feeling everything was hopeless to placing my hope in a toilet building.

The response was beyond my wildest dreams. Within 48 hours, we had received not only enough funding for the toilet building but were also able to replace half a school building, built with bamboo, straw, and mud that had crumbled to the ground due to termites.

The toilet project gave us momentum. The following month, Doreen and I took a trip to see some of our friends who had been personal supporters over the last 35 years. This visit resulted in *ServeNow's* first quarter ending up with almost $70,000 in income.

Today, the orphans at the schools in Uganda have increased to more than 4,000, and seven new school buildings have been completed!

The first projects take shape

Over the next year projects came to us in a variety of forms, as if God were opening doors and asked us to step through them. By the end of February, Maria and I received requests from two areas in India that had ended up in hopeless situations. Both projects in India had lost their funding overnight. There was a lot of dialogue back and forth, and it was decided that Maria and I would head to India in April to see what doors God had in mind to open for us.

We listened to the staff at the center in the Delhi slum called Sangam Vihar and were amazed at the crowdedness. In this area a million people live extremely close to one another, with their families and animals. Incredible traffic flows on narrow streets and alleyways.

Their work included children's meetings, Vacation Bible Schools, a small church, cell prayer groups to help Hindu women hear the Gospel, a tailoring school, a Sunday school in several locations every day of the week, and many other innovative programs where over 1,500 people heard the Gospel in one form or another every week! We said yes, and the cooperation began immediately. Their hopelessness in looking to the future turned to exuberant hope!

A similar story faced us when we arrived at the center in Kolkata. The activities in this tall, narrow, four-floor building were made up of preschool classes for children with a mostly Hindu background, as well as a day school for grades 1 through 4. Besides the schools for the children, there was also a drawing class, which

Their hopelessness in looking to the future turned to exuberant hope!

taught the children and youth the basics in art. Medical assistance was provided weekly so people could come and get free medical advice and medicines. A lawyer assisted those adults who could not read to fill in needed legal documents, and the lawyer explained the people's legal rights as those who live on the streets are often taken advantage of.

The children were learning to pray to Jesus! The tailoring school was training women in dire need of a trade. Many of these young women would easily have been caught up in trafficking, even being sold by their parents to get some family income. By learning a trade these women suddenly have more value than being sold in trafficking! The beautician school was also up and running, and this was another way to keep the young girls away from trafficking while teaching them a trade. While we were amazed at all these activities, the leader explained that there also was a need to start a computer training course. As in Delhi, we said yes to the request for working together, and suddenly *ServeNow* had added two strong programs in Delhi and Kolkata.

In October that year I spoke at the graduation for the tailoring school at the Kolkata center. The best student award went to a young lady. Noticing scars on her hands, feet, and face, I talked to her after the ceremony and heard an amazing story:

> My husband's family accused my family for not providing enough dowry, so my husband's family doused me with gasoline and set me on fire. I managed to subdue the fire, grabbed my son, and fled. I have now healed and enrolled in this class because I need to learn a trade to make a living and support my son. But most of all, I have found a new friend in Jesus Christ!

Through a generous partner we were able to set this lady up with a sewing machine, enough material to start a business and training in basic business principles.

The Basic Series *is born*

Our next stop was Hyderabad, where our friend Supratim lives. A month earlier Supratim had resigned from his previous work, and we invited him to head up the work in India, a decision we have never regretted. In anticipation of our visit, he had arranged for a pastors' seminar for a day. For weeks I had been wondering about how to meet a major need I had become aware of, not only in India but in other countries as well. Many of the pastors, especially in the rural areas, have very little, if any, training. Often their teaching tends to be more experiential than expounding biblical text. That meant that the congregations in turn lacked some basic teaching. I wondered if it would help if we provided them with some very basic biblical training in small doses.

As I prepared for the trip, I studied the life of Jesus and took many notes. The result was a simple 32-page pamphlet that I called *The Basic Things You Need to Know About Jesus*. As ServeNow didn't have any capital for publishing, I borrowed some money, sent the booklet for translation into the language spoken in Hyderabad, which is Telugu, and asked Supratim to print 1,000 copies, which I would pay for. We also did the same for Ukraine, where we also printed 1,000 copies in Russian.

When we broke for lunch at the pastors' meeting, we handed the booklets to all of them. Most everyone was asking for more copies for their church members, and most of the copies were gone that day. As the pastors looked at the booklet and read some of it, they came up to me and exclaimed, "This is what we need! But we need more subjects explained in this basic form. When can we receive more booklets on those subjects?"

When I returned home, I could not get their words out of my head! Basic truth . . . in small doses. How could I make that work? And how would it be funded? Taking a shower one day, all the pieces came together, and I rushed out of the shower, got dressed and ran to my computer. As fast as I

> When I returned home, I could not get their words out of my head! Basic truth . . . in small doses.

could, I wrote down single words of subjects that were essential for a Christian, such as reading the Bible, prayer, the meaning of salvation, God, the Holy Spirit, the Church, etc. My first list included 28 subjects, which later was enlarged to a total of 30 booklets. This would mean that if we could write them fast enough, translate them, produce them at speed, and have churches willing to work with us, there would be a major impact for the discipleship of the church members. We designed a program where each member in the church would receive a new booklet every three months. It would take seven and a half years for everyone to get each one of them.

Today it's happening! All 30 booklets, plus an extra one, dealing with emotions during the COVID-19 pandemic, have resulted in a strong discipleship training program with an impact I haven't seen before in more than 50 years of ministry! The booklets are now available in 23 languages with more languages in translation. Thousands of people are coming to faith, other churches experience old fashioned "revival," and people have been mobilized for community service, while the local church has grown on an average of more than 40 percent year after year! People from India, Ukraine, Africa, Latin America, Britain, and the United States helped to write the material, each booklet being 32 pages and using a fairly easy language level.

A slow start in Ukraine eventually takes on rocket speed

Maria and I left India and spent a few days in Ukraine. For years I had been privileged to work in Crimea, which at this time still belonged to Ukraine, and Maria and her children had all participated in summer camps there. However for this visit, we were invited to Dnepropetrovsk, Poltava, and Kharkiv in Central and Eastern Ukraine. We met pastors from many different denominations, held some seminars and shared *The Basic Things You Need to Know About Jesus* in Russian, which was still the most-used language in this part of Ukraine. There was a lot of enthusiasm for it, and one pastor exclaimed, "I need 1,000 copies just for my city; it's the best evangelistic tool I can imagine!"

Maria and I also had the opportunity to speak at two very different events. Maria presented to a group of secular women at a fashion show, and I addressed a group of secular businesspeople in a luxury men's clothing store during an open house. It was a stark contrast as we talked about ministry to the underprivileged, in an environment that obviously served the most privileged in this city's society.

Two of my closest friends from Crimea, Andrey and Tanya Shpygunov, drove all the way to Kharkiv, some 500 miles, to meet with Maria and me. They were still working with a center on the peninsula and had no plans to do anything else. Our passion for mission was so similar, and our friendship so deep, but there was no way imaginable for any cooperation for the future—except that Maria suggested she would like to work on some projects for Crimean women in crisis.

It seemed we had come to a dead end as far as moving forward in Ukraine. Ten months later Russia occupied Crimea and annexed it to Russia. The center where the Shpygunovs worked was closed, and Christian work was no longer possible. All the staff members were laid off. In the fall of 2014 I carefully inquired if the Shpygunovs would consider leaving Crimea, now under Russian control, and move somewhere close to Kiev, the capital of Ukraine. They responded positively. For five years in a row, the work in Ukraine has exploded under their leadership, from summer camps in the Carpathian Mountains, to a bakery school to cosmetology training. They have also reached out to people in the war zone, providing medical equipment that was donated from Sweden, which will be used in orphanages and hospitals. In addition the Shpygunovs work with young women in the Roma villages, as well as translating and distributing *The Basic Series* in both Russian and Ukrainian to the Roma community. And it all started with the meeting in Kharkiv, where we saw no or very little hope for the future of *ServeNow* in Ukraine.

God's Word for God's new people

On average, 63,500 new churches are established around the world every year.[1] In the past few years approximately 6,300 churches have been established every year in India by many different church-planting organizations.[2] The churches in India alone represent approximately one million new believers a year. However, many of these churches began with one man or woman being won to Christ in their village. While they previously were Hindus, Buddhists, Muslims, or Animists, they became fervent believers after hearing the Gospel and began sharing their new-found faith with others.

While these new believers came to Christ through hearing the Word of God declared, very few of these new believers had ever held a copy of the Bible in their own language. Many of the elderly cannot read, but the younger generation in each family can, and a New Testament in their language would go a long way. The growth of new churches is continuing month after month, but few, if any, understandable Scriptures are provided for these new believers.

> While these new believers came to Christ through hearing the Word of God declared, very few of these new believers had ever held a copy of the Bible in their own language.

One of the early steps for *ServeNow* was to take on the challenge to remedy this hopeless situation and provide as many new believers as possible in India with the Word of God over the next few years. As a result of this desire, God's Word for God's New People was launched. Together with the first *Basic Series* booklet, we attempted to provide a New Testament in the new believer's language. When understandable translations were not available, *ServeNow* printed small editions to make them available and provide hope through God's Word.

Garibay was a Hindu, and many years ago someone gave him a New Testament in an old, difficult translation. He didn't understand it. Coming into contact with a pastor, who explained the Word, Garibay came to faith and was baptized. He went away to Bible college for a while, and when he returned, he launched a church in a Hindu neighborhood. Today the church has 45 new believers and 60 children who hear the Gospel preached every Sunday. Garibay said, "The New Testaments *ServeNow* provided have done wonders in this church!"

A church in Odisha (a state in India) is situated right in the middle of an area that has been heavily persecuted since 2007. It was started 25 years ago with nothing and has now grown to 150 adults and 25 children. What was missing was New Testaments. The New Testaments provided in the Odia language gave these members new hope, and they in turn began to share the Gospel.

Another pastor felt a call to start a church in one of the most hopeless environments in India, right in the center of a garbage dump. When we told him that he may receive New Testaments and *The Basic Series* booklets, he exclaimed with tears in his eyes, "It would be like God sending me help to have these materials!" A few months later this man shared a hopeless situation for which he saw no solution. The primitively constructed church on the garbage dump had only a mud floor, and during the heavy rain season, the women could not sit down, as they all normally sit on the floor. Their clothes would be completely spoiled. A cement floor would make the difference, but how on earth could he pay for expensive cement? Within a short time *ServeNow* turned a hopeless situation to one of great hope, as a partner provided the funds to be able to pay for the needed bags of cement. Now the church members can sit down in any kind of weather!

In October 2013 I visited India together with a small team who had an opportunity to see for themselves the effectiveness of the God's Word for God's New People program. One Sunday, the team traveled several hours to the outskirts of Kolkata. The church we visited was constructed every Sunday of plastic curtains and tarps hung around the pastor's courtyard. Some 300 people gathered to hear the teaching from the Word and to receive a New Testament. Chaos almost broke out as we realized that while the congregation understood Bengali, they had three different mother tongues: Hindi, Odia, and Bengali. Fortunately, we were equipped with Scriptures in all three!

Later that week we took a two-hour car journey on bumpy roads until we reached the village church out "in nowhere." It was 4:00 p.m. on a weekday, and we wondered if anyone would be in church at that time. To our amazement the church was packed. In the courtyard outside there were just as many people as inside. Through an interpreter, I preached in the church about the importance of the Word of God. The pastor stood in the courtyard doorway and repeated what the interpreter said to those outside! When it was time to present the Word of God, both young and old were eager to get their copies and pushed and shoved to get them as soon as possible. There is no better hope for our lives than to receive and read the Word of God.

Winter coverings

Every winter the temperature drops below freezing in Northern India and Nepal. In the rural areas and the slums of the major cities, little children run around wearing hardly anything. At the same time, the parents and grandparents don't have enough clothes to keep warm, and many die every year because of the cold weather. When asked what is needed most this coming winter, the local people answered, "Socks! Then knitted hats, gloves, scarves, and sweaters. Then we also need warm wool blankets!"

The idea for a project like this began some eight years before when I received a phone call from a young lady we had provided some training for in the United States. "Lars, this is urgent," Sheeba explained in an agitated way, "We need to provide sweaters and blankets to the people. In the village I am in right now, it's below freezing, and people have nothing to keep them warm."

"Oh, Sheeba," I said, "you have so many clothes, just give them some of your own!"

"You don't understand," she continued, sounding exasperated, "This is not for a few, it's for an entire village! You need to help!"

That resulted in a project sending clothes and blankets that lasted for years. The full effect became clear to me many years later when I visited that village and we held a one-day meeting for some of the local pastors in the area. Sitting next to a pastor who spoke a little English, I asked him how he had started in ministry. He looked at me and said something I will never forget:

> Several years ago, Christians in this village came to my village and handed out blankets and New Testaments. I was an ardent Hindu, but as these were gifts, I accepted both and thanked them. I began reading the book, and Jesus transformed my life. Soon I began sharing the Gospel with others in the village and after some time I became their pastor!

Imagine if I had not responded to the call from Sheeba many years earlier!

As we launched *ServeNow* in India and Nepal, we found the same need still existed, and we were able to begin shielding young and old from the bitter cold. Many of these people had no hope of surviving the winter, and they now received a blanket or a sweater, a jacket, some pants, as well as caps, which were often provided by people in the United States who had knitted them.

To meet this need, we launched the support project in the United States to place a glass mason-type jar in their homes or office or give it to a friend. By filling the jar of change we could average $50 to $60 per jar, which a few years ago would pay for materials for 8 to 10 people. We provided them jar labels and lids, with a slit for the money. It took so little to provide so much hope!

It's hard for us Westerners to understand what a blessing this is for these people. But when it's 26 degrees Fahrenheit outside, and as cold inside, we know it makes a difference, especially when the "inside" consists of a tarp over two poles.

After we had launched *ServeNow*'s winter covering project, Sheeba sent me the following e-mail:

India is a country of villages and about 50 percent of the villages have very poor socio-economic conditions. The Indian population is said to be the melting pot of various races. Especially in rural India where various tribes and castes basically shy away from contact with the community at large. They endure geographical isolation and, of course, live in some rather backward conditions. Their everyday struggle for existence is too much as most of them live below the poverty line. It is believed that 75 percent of the population of India live in villages. One of the problems that rural India fights is "COLD" during the winter season. In many parts of India the majority of poor people die due to lack of enough warm coverings. Older and young are the main victims of this season. In many parts of the country it's below freezing where the people walk and sleep with a few layers of non-wool fabric. *ServeNow* can work as a great tool for fixing the below poverty winter problem by providing warmth. For the children we have selected wool socks, sweaters, wool scarves, knitted gloves and knitted hats as well as blankets, and for the adults wool blankets. Now is the time to respond to the need of people who are waiting to face the challenge of the cold months. If we do not act now it could be never for these precious people because the death rate increases every year, especially in the rural India. So, let's serve NOW!

Medical clinics

During the beginning period of *ServeNow,* one pastor in India contacted the India office and explained that no one in their village had ever seen a doctor. The India staff, probably anticipating that this was a one-time opportunity, provided a doctor to the village the following week. That day he saw more than 100 patients, who were from various religious backgrounds. Others were not ill, but they came to literally "see" the doctor! A table full of medicine became the pharmacy. Most illnesses were limited to diabetes and water-related illnesses, such as worms in the intestines. At another table, church members offered to pray for the patients. They also handed out the booklet about the great Physician, *The Basic Things You Need to Know About Jesus.*

> If we do not act now, it could be never for these precious people because the death rate increases every year.

Today many medical clinics are held each year in India and Nepal, providing hope when there is no medical help, and at the same time introduce these people without hope to the only hope in the world—Jesus Christ.

What started in a hopeless situation for me personally in the fall of 2012, turned into hope for literally thousands of people around the world within the next year. And it all began with a toilet!

5

Hope and a Future

"For I know the plans I have for you," declares the LORD,
"plans to prosper you and not to harm you, plans to give you
hope and a future."
—Jeremiah 29:11

Let me be the first to note my reluctance to begin this chapter by quoting this verse. Some of you, maybe like me, might be annoyed at how this verse is so often pulled out of context and used to say, "God has nothing but a wonderful plan for your life." The reality, however, is that life is full of challenges, trials, tribulation, pain, suffering, setbacks, and difficulties. Things do not always go well. Bad things happen. As John Eldredge notes, "There is just enough goodness to rouse our hearts with expectation, and plenty enough sadness to cut us back down."[1]

Our ultimate hope is not in this short earthly life, rather it's in the eternal life and hope we have in Christ. Our hope lies in a new heaven and new earth when God makes all things new (Revelation 21). Our hope is in Jesus and his coming (1 Thessalonians 4:17).

One of my favorite verses is, in fact, Titus 2:11-14, which states:

For the grace of God has appeared that offers salvation to all
people. It teaches us to say "No" to ungodliness and worldly
passions, and to live self-controlled, upright and godly lives in

this present age, while we wait for the blessed hope—the appearing of the glory of our great God and Savior, Jesus Christ, who gave himself for us to redeem us from all wickedness and to purify for himself a people that are his very own, eager to do what is good.

That said, I have also come to see how God is at work in extraordinary ways to give people hope and a future here on earth. They are glimpses of our full hope and eternal future even now on earth. And tying in with the last part of that passage in Titus, Jesus died not just to save us for eternity, but to cause us to be eager to do what is good right here and now! Jesus right now is setting the captives free and working to transform people's lives and situations.

Hope for one turned into hope for many

Years ago, Tanya—our director in Ukraine—met a young girl who grew up being moved from orphanage to orphanage. At one point, she began to cut her hair like a boy, dress like a boy, walk like a boy, and act like a boy. When asked why, she explained that it was because she noticed how many of her friends were being raped and ended up in human trafficking and prostitution. This is a vicious cycle in Ukraine. Some children have even been labeled as "mentally retarded," even though they are not, simply to ensure these students are not allowed to attend school. As a result, they do not learn many practical skills, and once they are 18, they are on their own. Approximately 80 percent end up with meager paying jobs, go into prostitution, become trapped in human trafficking, or turn to drugs and alcohol; many eventually commit suicide.

When Tanya heard this, she was compelled to do something for girls like this to give them hope and a future. This became the inspiration for a bakery program that *ServeNow* initiated in

Ukraine. It's aimed at young girls just like the one Tanya had spoken with. Through this program, many young girls are indeed finding hope and a future.

Hope in the garbage dump

I personally observed this at the graduation ceremony of *Serve-Now's* first bakery class in South Asia. We hosted this training in a slum area next to a garbage dump, where many of the women in this village worked long and hard hours sorting through the dump to find items they could sell to a middleman. This middleman would make a lot of money, while the women received the leftovers, which they tried to survive on. Besides being a low-paying job, it's also an occupation associated with shame and social stigma. I will never forget sitting there on the day of their graduation, facing their beaming faces. I was so impressed to hear that beyond the skill itself, the bakery course had given them confidence and self-worth, and it also restored their dignity. One mother shared how her children had been ashamed of her because of her job. But because of the training offered by *ServeNow*, they were now proud of her! Even more than the training itself, this was what meant the most to her.

Another one of the graduates shared, "I see this opportunity as a ray of hope which will enable me to help my sisters in their education and in their marriages. Thank you for helping create a brighter future for myself and my sisters!"

When I take part in graduation ceremonies like that, I almost always find myself sharing this promise from the book of Jeremiah. God's promise is to give his people hope and a future as they seek him. It relates to God's purpose for Israel on earth, as well as pointing to eternity. That becomes fitting and relatable to so many today because the Israelites found themselves as captives in Babylon, having lost their homeland as well as their dignity.

God was promising restoration to them. He was promising them a future and hope so they could endure the situation they found themselves in until he restored them.

It's hope that keeps us going

Hope is like the air we breathe. It's essential for life. We cannot survive, let alone thrive, without it. Hope is what has kept me going in many challenging situations in the past. But let me also remind you that hope is different than hope realized.

In Romans 8:23-25, the apostle Paul writes about that:

> *Not only so, but we ourselves, who have the firstfruits of the Spirit, groan inwardly as we wait eagerly for our adoption to sonship, the redemption of our bodies. For in this hope we were saved. But hope that is seen is no hope at all. Who hopes for what they already have? But if we hope for what we do not yet have, we wait for it patiently.*

In Hebrews 11:1, we are further told that *faith is confidence in what we hope for and assurance about what we do not see.* The next verse also reminds us that this is what the ancients were commended for. The rest of chapter 11 in the book of Hebrews gives us example after example and story after story of men and women who lived by faith and therefore pleased God. Ultimately, none of them had their hope fully realized. However, many of them did experience what I would call "down payments" of promises given.

The point is this: Much of our lives we live in the in-between of hope and hope realized, and even when hope is achieved, it's never fully realized in light of what God has planned for us in eternity. This is an important principle, because it's hope that spurs us onward even when what we are hoping for has not yet come to pass.

My hope came alive and was realized

Let me share a personal example from my life and promises I believe God has given *ServeNow*. Ten years before I joined *ServeNow*, and before it even existed, God laid on my heart a desire to one day lead an international mission organization that would make the dreams and prayers of others a reality. When our founder, Lars Dunberg, approached me about *ServeNow*, we spent about three hours together at a Denny's restaurant, where he shared in great detail about all the aspects of the ministry of *ServeNow*. As we talked, I suddenly remembered a document that I had written 10 years earlier. When I finally returned home that evening, I dug the document up from an old computer. When I compared it with what *ServeNow* was doing and its model of partnering with national leaders, it was eerily similar, even down to specific projects and countries!

I share this story because over the years it has been experiences like that, linked with specific promises in God's Word, which have kept me going through difficult situations. These promptings, stirrings, leadings, desires, visions, dreams—whatever you want to call them—are about the future and a hope. They provide motivation, inspiration, perseverance, endurance, and focus.

It's truly amazing and exhilarating when some of those hopes are realized! Soon after I had been appointed the president of *ServeNow*, I spent five days with our national directors and basically put one question before them: "If money were not an issue, what would you really do in your countries?" As we began to dream and pray without being tied down by current realities, hope began to rise. As I later worked with Lars to put all those dreams together with real numbers, resulting in a three-year plan with another three-year plan to follow, I thought, *You know, this isn't as impossible as it may have seemed!* What was that? It was hope!

As we put the plan on paper and began to share it with people, having no idea how we would possibly see it fulfilled, we noted the most significant breakthrough we had experienced within that first year. At perhaps my lowest, most discouraged point, I began drafting some e-mails to partners to see if they could help us out. I was just "hoping" to make up some lost ground. But within five minutes of e-mailing the first couple, the phone rang, and I saw on the caller ID that it was that couple. I nervously picked up, said hello, and they asked me how much money we needed. After beating around the bush for a few minutes, I finally threw out a number that was more than they had given to date within one year. And then I heard the news that altered everything. They responded by saying, "Well, we have had a great year this year in our business. And we have been praying for some time about something we felt God was putting on our hearts. We were going to give you a significant gift year-end, but if you want to, we can begin giving it now." The amount they were suggesting giving was four times the amount I had suggested to them. It was an answer to a wild prayer we had been praying for during the past several years. That was significant, too, because the entire fiscal year before, our total income was not much more than that! It was essentially a gift that enabled us to double our impact!

Hope breeds more hope

While it was exciting to receive such good news, I was teaching at a pastor's conference in Uganda a couple of months later when God began challenging me further. During worship, God started to put new hope in my heart. He basically began challenging me not to be content with that gift. Instead, he allowed that gift to increase my faith and propel me to believe him for even 10 times to fulfill other dreams, prayers, hopes, and promises around the world! Once again, I am looking forward in hope to what God has for *ServeNow* in the future. In fact, what God has done in the past should encourage our hearts in the present and give us greater confidence for the future!

God has placed desires on all our hearts and that is why I share these stories. It's true that not every desire may be from him. But many are indeed.

I remember when I first came back to the Lord. For the first time, I read the promise in Psalm 37:4, which says, *Take delight in the* LORD, *and he will give you the desires of your heart.* At the time, I had just given up my greatest passion in life up to that

> **What God has done in the past, should encourage our hearts in the present and give us greater confidence for the future!**

point, which was to become a major league baseball player! When I realized God was calling me to surrender that desire since it was not his desire for my life, I was lost as to what he had in mind for my future. But as I simply began to delight myself in him, he began to place new desires—his desires—on my heart and chart my future for me. Ironically, at the same time I had just started a Bible study with youth my age. The one girl I was desperately in love with and could not get over even after she broke up with me in 11th grade started coming to that Bible study with her sister. To cut a long story short, that was how Lauren and I ended up getting back together, eventually married, and had four beautiful children!

Another generation's hope influences the future

Psalm 37:4 also happened to be Lauren's grandfather's favorite verse as well. Let me tell you his story because it intersects not only with my life but also with our founder and *ServeNow.*

My wife's grandfather grew up during the Great Depression in rural Pennsylvania. He was from a Mennonite farming family, but he had ambitions early on in life, itching for something much different. At that time, many preachers only spoke about being called into ministry as pastors or missionaries. Still, he felt called to be a businessman and an entrepreneur. In fact, his prayer at age 15 was to give away one million dollars someday for the sake of the Gospel. That was a truly remarkable and somewhat crazy prayer when considering the circumstances, as this was in the 1930s!

However, he did become a businessman and entrepreneur and launched a family-owned and operated snack-food company called Herr's. Today Herr's is being run by various members of the second-generation who are handing it off to the third generation! It's now the largest family-operated snack food company in the United States.[2]

But this is what is wild. Lauren's grandfather's success gained notable recognition over the years, and he was incredibly faithful in giving generously. So much so, that he gave away far more than his initial prayer. The single one-time largest check from a partner Lars has received in any organization came from him! If it were not for him and his wife and their faithfulness and long-term relationship with our founder, I would never have met Lars. Thus, I would never have ended up leading *ServeNow*! It's incredible how the dreams God puts on our hearts have long-term implications that affect and intersect even with future generations long into the future!

What dreams has God put in your heart?

The question is what has God put on your heart? What future and hope does he have for you? What desires is he stirring within you? At the time of writing this chapter, a partner of *ServeNow* who is a strong prayer warrior sent me an e-mail. She attended the church I pastored in New Jersey. I shared with her how this book was born out of an intense desire I felt God put on my heart. She replied with a verse from Philippians 2:13, which states, *For it is God who works in you to will and to act in order to fulfill his good purpose.* Before God brings anything into outward expression, he works inwardly to inspire those actions. God is the One who stirs holy desire and divine motivation and inspiration as well as action and good deeds! This is where the Christian life really becomes exciting!

One of the dreams I presently hold is a shared dream expressed by some of the girls who grew up as orphans in Uganda. Over the years, they have been a part of our teams by helping us get around and taking care of various needs. As I began to know them, they shared that they want to start a trade school where they can teach skills to vulnerable young men and women who don't want go to college but want to work with their hands. They have a dream to teach tailoring and cosmetology for the women and mechanics for the boys. It's a huge dream and quite expensive, but I believe with all my heart that they need

> Let me ask you once again, what is God stirring in your heart? What is the future and hope he has in store for you while you're still on earth?

to experience God's faithfulness in their lives for their generation. So, in hope, I am believing with them for God to provide for this Trade School dream.

Let me ask you once again, what is God stirring in your heart? What is the future and hope he has in store for you while you're still on earth?

I love the apostle Paul's prayer in Ephesians 1:18-20 and want to pray it over you to close this chapter:

> *I pray that the eyes of your heart may be enlightened in order that you may know the hope to which he has called you, the riches of his glorious inheritance in his holy people, and his incomparably great power for us who believe. That power is the same as the mighty strength he exerted when he raised Christ from the dead and seated him at his right hand in the heavenly realms.*

6

Renewing our Hope

The LORD is the everlasting God,
the Creator of the ends of the earth.
He will not grow tired or weary,
and his understanding no one can fathom.
He gives strength to the weary
and increases the power of the weak.
—Isaiah 40:28-29

No matter our age or what we have experienced of God thus far in life, it's no secret that we all grow weary at times. Life takes its toll on us and can wear us down. Over time, circumstances and situations can constantly chip away and rob us of peace and joy and hope. We all go through valleys in life and sometimes wonder if we will ever stand upon the mountaintop again. We may go through seasons of feelings like we are forgotten, overlooked, or just grinding through another day. Young and old both experience this in different ways. All of us have those moments when we need our hope renewed. In the next pages, I will provide some spiritual practices and practical tips on renewing our hope.

All of us have those moments when we need our hope renewed.

The first key to renewing our hope

Isaiah 40:26-31 offers several keys for renewing hope. The first key passage is found in verses 26:

Lift up your eyes and look to the heavens:
Who created all these?
He who brings out the starry host one by one
and calls forth each of them by name.
Because of his great power and mighty strength,
not one of them is missing.

This key is remembering who God is and refocusing on him as Creator. This passage begins with a reminder that not a day or night goes by where God fails to bring out the starry host one by one and calls forth each of them by name. It reminds us that because of his great power and mighty strength, not one of them is missing.

Why is this important to renewing our hope? It's because what causes us to lose hope so often is feeling abandoned or forgotten. Under the inspiration of the Holy Spirit, the prophet Isaiah puts forward the inner thoughts we, even as God's people, sometimes struggle with and asks in light of this truth:

Why do you complain, Jacob?
Why do you say, Israel,
"My way is hidden from the LORD;
my cause is disregarded by my God"?
Do you not know?
Have you not heard?
The LORD is the everlasting God,
the Creator of the ends of the earth. (Isaiah 40:27-18)

We need to be reminded of this truth often. If the God who created the universe, knows and calls forth every star in the sky—as well as knows the number of hairs on our heads, which implies he knows every little detail about our lives—then how in the world could he forget us? He is the everlasting God, the Creator of the ends of the earth!

ServeNow's India staff leaders visited a community deep inside the jungles of North Bengal, India, to bring them blankets for the winter and share the Good News of the Gospel. The pastor we were partnering with told us the following incredible story:

> This village is so remote that we hardly get to see any people from the outside visit us. There are no bus services or cars to this village nor do any cellphones work here. There are only two vehicles that come to this community once a week on Mondays with weekly supplies, as there is no store here. This is a place ignored by the government, politicians, and people in general. We are very happy to have *ServeNow* here and to receive these warm blankets to keep us warm in the chilly nights. I recently lost my father—who was struck by lightning—because I could not take him to the hospital, which is situated at least an hour and a half drive away. On that fateful night there were no vehicles available, nor any doctors or any health workers available. We could not save our father and even if there had been a vehicle available, chances were small that he would survive the one-hour drive through the forest trail, which is one of the bumpiest rides in the region. Today I am blessed to host *ServeNow* in my home and my community. You are encouraging us with the message that even when we think we have been ignored by everyone, there is a God who remembers our needs. I am happy that many in the community could hear about Jesus today and I hope that many may come to know the Lord through *ServeNow*'s winter covering distribution today.

The Creator of the universe remembers us wherever we may be and no matter how forgotten we may feel! This is a truly amazing reality. Together with the psalmist, we can echo his sentiment in Psalm 8:3-4, *When I consider your heavens, the work of your fingers, the moon and the stars, which you have set in place, what is mankind that you are mindful of them, human beings that you care for them?*

When I am feeling down and discouraged, spending time in the outdoors in God's creation is like medicine to my soul. God even did this with Abraham! When Abraham was struggling with God's promise to him, God brought him outside and told him to look up at the stars. As Abraham gazed to the sky God repeated his promise. It was there and then Abraham believed God! There is something about creation that restores our faith in our Creator, renews our hope, and heals our innermost beings.

> The Creator of the universe remembers us wherever we may be, and no matter how forgotten we may feel!

I have been privileged to grow up in the rolling farmland of Lancaster County, Pennsylvania, pastored a church along the Jersey Shore in New Jersey, and now live in the beautiful state of Colorado near the Rocky Mountains. It's amazing what a day in the mountains, on a beach, or on a hike can do for the soul in renewing your outlook and hope in life! Even if you cannot do those things, take a walk or step outside at night and gaze at the stars. Our Creator's work has a healing quality to it!

When the apostle John received a vision of things to come in the book of Revelation, he wrote the following about the new heaven and new earth to come:

> *On each side of the river stood the tree of life, bearing twelve crops of fruit, yielding its fruit every month. And the leaves of the tree are for the healing of the nations. No longer will there*

be any curse. The throne of God and of the Lamb will be in the city, and his servants will serve him. (Revelation 22:2-3)

God has designed nature to be healing! In fact, many of the old hymns frequently incorporated lyrics dealing with creation. Here's the story behind "How Great Thou Art."

> If you have heard two hymns in your life, chances are you have heard "How Great Thou Art." In terms of popularity, it is generally considered second only to "Amazing Grace". . . The beloved hymn didn't start its life as a song. It began as a poem, a Swedish poem at that.
>
> In 1885, Carl Boberg, a Swedish editor and future politician, was walking home . . . A thundercloud appeared on the horizon. Lightning flashed. Thunderclaps shook the air, sending Boberg running for shelter.
>
> When the storm began to relent, he rushed home. He opened his windows to let in the fresh bay air, and the vision of tranquility that greeted him stirred something deep in his soul. The sky had cleared. Thrushes sang, and in the distance, the resonant knell of church bells sounded. With the juxtaposition between the roaring thunderstorm and such bucolic calm as background, Boberg sat down and wrote "O Store Gud"—the poem that, through a winding series of events would become "How Great Thou Art."[1]

The poem was set to the music of a Swedish folk song, and some 50 years later an English version appeared in Great Britain. In 1954 the song found an audience in the United States and became the signature song for the Billy Graham Evangelistic Association.

Let's look at the wonderful lyrics of "How Great Thou Art" which were inspired by Psalm 8:

> O Lord my God, when I in awesome wonder,
> Consider all the worlds Thy hands have made;

I see the stars, I hear the rolling thunder,
Thy power throughout the universe displayed

Then sings my soul, My Savior God, to Thee,
How great Thou art, How great Thou art.
Then sings my soul, My Savior God, to Thee,
How great Thou art, How great Thou art!

When through the woods, and forest glades I wander,
And hear the birds sing sweetly in the trees.
When I look down, from lofty mountain grandeur
And hear the brook, and feel the gentle breeze.

Then sings my soul, My Savior God, to Thee,
How great Thou art, How great Thou art.
Then sings my soul, My Savior God, to Thee,
How great Thou art, How great Thou art![2]

A basic lesson from Job

When I think of this hymn, I also think about the book of Job
and how God handled Job's despair. Like Job, we so often ask the
"Why?" question. Usually, this is related to personal suffering and
the painful realities of life in this fallen world. Most of the book
of Job contains his anguish and examines his thoughts as he wres-
tles with his seemingly unfair suffering. Over and over Job cries
out "Why God?" and asks for a hearing. However, God is silent
through most of the book, which amplifies Job's suffering.

Let me briefly note a powerful insight on this point. God's silence is not the same as God's absence. God's silence is evidence of
his loving presence. I say that because Job's friends were a comfort
to him initially during the first week when they simply sat with
him in silence and entered his suffering and sorrow.

However, when they opened their mouths and began to make
various theological cases, they ended up adding to Job's suffering

with their words! They would have done better to remain silent and just continue to share in Job's suffering. Isn't that so true? In an effort to comfort, we think we have to say something, but usually our platitudes don't help.

When God finally does speak to Job, he never answers Job's "Why?" questions. Instead he reveals himself and reminds Job of who he is. God knows that answers usually do not help. Our "Why?" questions are more than questions. They are cries of anguish and

> **God's silence is not the same as God's absence.**

longing for relief or hope. Even when Jesus cried out, *My God, My God, why have you forsaken me?* (Matthew 27:46), he was not really looking for God, the Father, to remind him of the reason he was on the cross. Jesus knew why! And the "answer" would not change his levels of anguish, suffering, and pain.

Likewise, though we may ask "Why?," we are looking for something more than answers even if we think it is answers we need. We ask "Why?" but God reveals "who" he is. Hope is renewed through being reminded of who God is! Further, hope is not found in trying to figure out the why of our suffering. Rather, hope is found in looking beyond present suffering to God's promise and purpose in suffering. In his book, *Where Is God When It Hurts*, Philip Yancey writes, "To backward-looking questions of cause, to the 'Why?' questions, [Scripture] gives no definitive answer. But it does hold out hope for the future, that even suffering can be transformed or 'redeemed.'"[3] Our hope is renewed not by looking back at our past or even at our present circumstances. Hope is renewed by looking forward in faith to what God has promised beyond our suffering and despite whatever may have caused our suffering.

The second key to renewing our hope

The second key to renewing our hope is found in the last part of Isaiah 40. Let's look at it:

> *He will not grow tired or weary,*
> > *and his understanding no one can fathom.*
> *He gives strength to the weary*
> > *and increases the power of the weak.*
> *Even youths grow tired and weary,*
> > *and young men stumble and fall;*
> *but those who hope in the Lord*
> > *will renew their strength.*
> *They will soar on wings like eagles;*
> > *they will run and not grow weary,*
> *they will walk and not be faint.* (vv. 28-31)

This second key is to remember that while we may grow tired and weary, the God we serve does not, and he has promised that if we put our hope in him, he will renew our strength! In other words, to renew our hope, we must realign our hope, specifically in God. Just like a vehicle that experiences wear and tear as it's used and needs frequent tune-ups and realignments to function properly, so do we. This is not to admit failure. Rather, it is to admit we are not superhuman! A cellphone or computer requires being plugged in and recharged. As God's people, we also derive our strength from him. And the good news is, he never runs out of strength or energy! And he specifically promises to use his strength when we are weak and weary.

Sometimes, we experience false guilt. We feel guilty for being exhausted or emotionally drained. We think we should be able to maintain our joy, peace, and hope at all times. We feel we must be strong for others. However, this is neither biblical nor sustainable. God's promise of renewed strength, hope, peace, and joy is specifically reserved and available to those who recognize their need for it!

There is a strength and wisdom we can operate in that is not our own and does not require struggling and straining so hard to muster up or manufacture. It's a strength that comes from placing our hope in the Lord, rather than in our circumstances, feelings, ourselves, or other people. To renew our hope, we must put our hope in the Lord.

Psalm 42 can help us. In this psalm the psalmist is depressed. Yet he begins to "preach to himself" and remind himself to put his hope in God. Here's what he says to himself a couple times in this chapter: *Why, my soul, are you downcast? Why so disturbed within me? Put your hope in God for I will yet praise him, my Savior and my God* (v. 5).

Much has been said and published in recent years relating to emotional intelligence. A huge part of emotional intelligence is being aware of our own emotions. Before we can deal with our emotions, we have to acknowledge our emotions. Once we acknowledge our emotions, we can then begin to manage our emotions rather than letting them control us. As Daniel Goleman writes in his book, *Emotional Intelligence*: "All emotions are in essence, impulses to act . . . The very root of the word *emotion* is *motere*, the Latin verb 'to move,' plus the prefix 'e-' to connote 'move away,' suggesting that a tendency to act is implicit in every emotion."[4] In other words, when properly managed and channeled, emotions drive us to productive action. But when they manage and control us they often cripple or consume us in destructive ways.

Putting our hope in God and choosing to praise him is a powerful way to handle our feelings of despair, discouragement, depression, and loss of hope. It's typically the last thing we feel like doing, but it's a powerful weapon to regain perspective and renewing our hope.

Where we place our hope is critical

Where and in what and in whom we place our hope is critical. Our hope must be in God. And why not? Everything else in this world is temporary, limited, changing, and subject to decay. Only God is eternal, limitless, unchangeable, all wise, all powerful, and all loving! But sometimes we must speak this to ourselves and remind ourselves to realign ourselves and our hope in him.

I find it fascinating that even a well-known atheist, Matthew Parris, told *The Times* (London), "As an atheist, I truly believe Africa needs God."[5] And not long after returning from Africa, Matthew Parris gave another interview that is now often quoted:

> I've become convinced of the enormous contribution that Christian evangelism makes in Africa; sharply distinct from the work of secular NGOs, government projects and international aid efforts. These alone wills not do. Education and training alone will not do. In Africa, Christianity changes people's hearts. It brings a spiritual transformation. The rebirth is real. The change is good.[6]

I read this around the time *ServeNow* was beginning to work on expanding to more countries in Africa. We were exploring that idea because we were seeing the extraordinary impact the *Basic Series* booklets were having in Uganda, and there was a credible sense that these discipleship resources would have a similar impact in other countries. As a result, in September 2019, I traveled to three countries in West Africa where we launched the first French *Basic Series* booklet about Jesus. Not long afterward, I received this note from one of the coordinators that confirmed the observation in the quote above:

> I am very encouraged about the first launch! It gives me hope about the future. This launch has confirmed that *ServeNow*'s holistic approach is coming to Africa at the right time. It's

going to assist and empower our pastors in different local churches, even in the more remote and harder to reach places.

The key word here is once again *hope*. While *ServeNow* is involved in many different programs and projects, the one thing God is really providing to literally millions of people around the world is hope.

One project *ServeNow* helps with is a short video series in Arabic called *The Road to Paradise*. These videos are distributed through YouTube and other social media to millions of Arabic-speaking people throughout the Middle East, North Africa, and Europe. The testimonies that pour in from the viewers are ones that really speak of the longing for true hope.

Many shared reactions like this one: "The way the program presented the topics was irresistible, so the viewers found themselves searching more and discovered that there is no paradise except through Jesus Christ." Others stated, "The program makes sense and speaks to the mind and the heart together and does not insult Islam, and

> *ServeNow* is involved in many different programs and projects, the one thing God is really providing to literally millions of people around the world is hope.

that was what encouraged us to continue to watch the program and led us to accept Jesus Christ." Muslims around the world are looking for hope, and they are finding it in the Good News of the Gospel!

In chapter four, Lars shared how in Uganda, *ServeNow* is engaged in rebuilding school buildings for impoverished children so they can have an education. Why is this so important? Education is their basic ticket out of poverty, but without a school building they have no hope of such an education. The school buildings are more than buildings. They are symbols of hope!

One answer to hope leads to many more

Let me share with you a great testimony that has come from these school buildings *ServeNow* has helped rebuild. My very first trip to Uganda was with *ServeNow*. It was also the first "official" trip I took after joining the staff. Lars and I went together, and one day we were taken to one of the school locations that was in desperate need of school buildings. An intense storm had recently blown the roof off one of the buildings while the children were inside. Thankfully, no one was hurt, but these 20-year-old, mud-thatched, termite-infested, storm-destroyed classrooms were condemned by the government. As the principal took us on a tour of the school grounds, we stood on a pile of dirt where another building had completely collapsed because of termite infestation. As we stood there listening to the story, Lars felt the Lord speaking to him and telling him to "do something about this." So, when we had returned to our hotel, we debriefed together, and Lars suggested we would have a competition to see who could raise most money the fastest to rebuild this school building! It was a breakeven! We met the goal, and within a short time, while we were still there, we had enough money to rebuild half a school building!

That was simply the beginning of many more buildings to follow! Fast-forward about three years. I was once again visiting Uganda and this school location, where now several buildings had been rebuilt. As the national leader and I stepped out of the van, we were once again swarmed by hundreds of children, but it seemed like there were far more of them than the first time. Additionally, since these schools are located in remote areas, they serve as hub for the entire community. That's why there also is a church at this location. When Lars and I first visited, we also spoke at the church, which at that time was half built with no roof. It had gaping holes for windows and was half empty. However, I was surprised to see that this time the church building was completed, and when we went in to the service, it was packed with people and also full of life.

At that point, I leaned over to our director, Moses, and asked him several questions: Why were there more children at this school? How did they manage to finish building the church when *Serve-Now* had not provided any resources to do so? And why were there so many more people and energy compared to three years ago?

Moses' answer provided me with the most incredible testimony. When the schools began being built at this location by *Serve-Now,* the community began to take notice, because they knew that the children and the church members were praying for this. As a result, they began to see the hand of God and recognized that he must hear and answer the prayers of his people! More people began coming to the church, finding hope in Christ and experiencing God answering their prayers. And before we knew what had happened, they were able to finish building the church themselves!

Soon, word spread beyond the community. During the national elections, the President of Uganda, set up camp with his team at our school while campaigning in that area because word had reached the highest levels that these were the best built schools! In a touching manner, our partner in Uganda told me

> **People began to see the hand of God and recognized that he must hear and answer the prayers of his people!**

that years before he felt the Lord tell him that this school location would become a "city of God." However, right at the time when Lars and I first visited and stood on that pile of dirt, everyone was telling Moses to close this location down. But he felt like the Lord was telling him to "hold on" and "hang on" and not lose hope or heart. We did not know all this until after the fact. God had restored their hope and ours too!

And that is why we too can put our hope in the Lord. He has promised in Psalm 25:3, *No one who hopes in you will ever be put to shame.*

7

Hope in Times of Despair

When Judas, who had betrayed him, saw that Jesus was condemned, he was seized with remorse and returned the thirty pieces of silver to the chief priests and the elders. "I have sinned," he said, "for I have betrayed innocent blood."

"What is that to us?" they replied. "That's your responsibility."

So Judas threw the money into the temple and left. Then he went away and hanged himself.
—Matthew 27:3-5

This is one of the most haunting passages in Scripture. Additionally, suicide is becoming more and more of a tragic reality in our world today. Just a few hours before writing this chapter, I received a phone call informing me about the suicide of one of our supporting partners. When I was pastoring a church in New Jersey, a string of high school suicides befell the neighboring town. Many of the teens came from well-to-do family situations, were successful in school, and seemed to have a bright future.

I am also writing this chapter on the heels of what will be forever remembered as the COVID-19 months, when the world was shut down in an unprecedented way due to this virus. But one of the heart-wrenching realities worldwide associated with lockdown measures put in place was the rise and increase of suicides.[1]

Nepal for example, where suicide was already on the rise, experienced a surge due to the loss of hope during the COVID-19 virus and the lockdown.[2] In an African country, I was forwarded a picture of a man who committed suicide because he lost his job and could not provide for his family. He felt so ashamed that he could not live with himself anymore.

Other articles and authors have also pointed out the increase of suicides over the last two decades. The American Psychological Association for example noted the following:

> The increase in the rate of death by suicide in the United States between 2000 and 2016, from 10.4 to 13.5 per 100,000 people, according to a National Center for Health Statistics analysis of data from the National Vital Statistics System. The rate increased by about 1 percent per year from 2000 through 2006 and by about 2 percent per year from 2006 through 2016.[3]

As noted earlier, suicide can affect anyone, even those whose circumstances would otherwise suggest a "good life." We need to talk about suicide more, because it's an epidemic and a real struggle for so many. At its core, it's also a loss of hope.

There was a solution to Judas' despair

Let us dissect for a moment the story of Judas committing suicide. Judas hanged himself because he was so tormented by what he had done that he could no longer live with himself. Shame, guilt, and the reality of what his actions resulted in for Jesus coupled with the fact he could not undo what he had done drove him mad. While not true in every case of suicide, shame is often a factor. Shame that leads to suicide is ultimately a loss of hope in seeing any way out of a painful situation.

Beyond the tragedy of Judas' betrayal and suicide, something else haunts me even more. Had Judas held on a little longer, he would have seen that Jesus was being "hung" in his place and bearing the shame, guilt, and full consequences of his sin and our sin and the sin of the world. Jesus hung on a cross, so that we do not have to hang ourselves, spiritually or physically. He died, so that we might live. He suffered, so that we might be forgiven fully. He bled for us, that we might know we are loved, no matter what we have done.

I write this chapter with a deep aching in my heart and a prayer on my lips, that someone, anyone, might read this chapter and not go through with this action. Someone, anyone, might read this story and see that your story does not need to end this same way. Someone, anyone, might rediscover the hope of the Good News of what Jesus has done for you on the cross. He has carried your shame, so you do not have to. He has suffered for your sins, so that you do not have to. And there is hope, no matter how hopeless you may feel. Jesus does understand your pain. And he cares for you. Let him minister to you in his own way and time as he knows is best for you.

I will never forget a letter sent to me by someone who heard some of my sermons while I was pastoring in New Jersey, and I have it framed by my desk. In the first part of the letter she wrote, "There are no words that can express how very thankful I am for you and your sermons. I began to listen to them many months ago. It was a pivotal point in my life where I knew I was going to make a change in my life, or I was going to die. I was in a very dark place with no hope. Through your sermons God has brought

> There is hope, no matter how hopeless you may feel. Jesus does understand your pain. And he cares for you.

me to my knees, helped me to battle the enemy that was my mind, and eventually brought me to hope and salvation."

A solution to despair in Africa

Over the years, we have also received heart-wrenching and heart-touching stories of people in despair finding hope through *ServeNow*. One story I received had our staff and board shedding a few tears. Here is our coordinator in this African country sharing it in his own words.

> On Sunday, we normally go to the church together with my wife. But this special Sunday, my wife asked me to go ahead of her. Not knowing why at the time, we realized later why this was God's plan. On her way to church, she saw a man seated on the roadside crying with tears. When she stopped, the man begged her and said, 'Have pity on me, please give me something to eat, I am dying'. These words deeply touched my wife's heart. She did not hesitate, even for a moment. As they both talked, this was a beginning of new life. She realized that the man had lost his job due to COVID-19. He was not only hungry, but sick as well at the point of suicide, really desperate. The man had a family and didn't know what to do in life. My wife decided to go to his home and saw a lamentable situation of the man's family. She immediately gave the family some basic dry food and also bought appropriate medicine. Later I also went to visit this family and sat with the man. God is at work in the entire family. I discovered that the family had not eaten anything for the last three days. I was profoundly touched and cried in tears with the entire family. I had a golden opportunity to share the Word of God to the family. God is at work in a special way. The whole family, including the husband who was at the point of suicide when my wife met him, accepted the Lord. Really, I have no words to thank the Lord for

this compassionate work *ServeNow* has enabled to do to save many lives in special ways. This is a veritable compassionate work being done as Jesus would do and the fruit is visible.

This is not an isolated story. God is at work around the world to provide real and lasting hope!

Vital lessons in a story from the book of Joshua

In Joshua 7, there is a story of a man named Achan. In the story, Achan takes and hides plunder that was meant to belong only to the Lord. This man's sin affects the entire Israelite community to the point that they lose the next battle as a result; lives were lost. After a time of humbling themselves before the Lord, the Lord reveals this "sin in the camp" and calls the leaders to deal with it. Achan and his family are subsequently found out, taken to what becomes known as the Valley of Achor and stoned to death. It's a tragic story in Israel's history and became a place associated with shame and disgrace. In fact, Achor means "trouble" in Hebrew. It was a sober reminder to the Israelites that our sin never just affects us, but everyone around us, especially those closest to us. Sin has real consequences.

But the story does not end here. Years later, a word came forth through two different prophets—Isaiah and Hosea—that God was going to revisit the Valley of Achor and do a work of transformation. In Isaiah 65:10 this prophetic word is given, *Sharon will become a pasture for flocks, and the Valley of Achor a resting place for herds, for my people who seek me.* In Hosea 2:14-16, God begins speaking hope over his wayward people and says:

> *Therefore I am now going to allure her;*
> *I will lead her into the wilderness*
> *and speak tenderly to her.*

> *There I will give her back her vineyards*
> *and will make the Valley of Achor a door of hope.*
> *There she will respond as in the days of her youth,*
> *as in the day she came up out of Egypt.*
> *In that day," declares the Lord,*
> *"you will call me 'my husband';*
> *you will no longer call me 'my master.' "*

The promise here is that God is going to remove the shame associated with this place and entirely transform its reputation in a way that it will become a place where people will experience hope and find healing!

So, the question is "How and when and where was this accomplished?" These are the only two Scripture references that speak of the Valley of Achor, apart from Joshua 7. I believe the answer lies in a little detail found in that chapter. In verse 1, we are told that Achan was the son of Karmi, the son of Zimri, the son of Zerah, of the tribe of Judah. What is so important about that? The line of Judah already had a soiled reputation. In Genesis 37, you will find that Judah was the brother who had the idea to sell Joseph into slavery. After they took this action against their own brother, the next chapter of Genesis goes on to focus on Judah's next season of life . . . and it's not pretty! For one thing, he left his family and married a Canaanite, indicating a walking away from the faith of his fathers. Judah started a family there and finally found a wife, Tamar, for his firstborn son. However, Judah's son was so wicked in God's sight that the Lord put him to death! So Judah told his next son to sleep with his brother's wife and fulfill his responsibility to carry on his brother's line. However, this son, did not sleep with his brother's wife and ensured she would not get pregnant by him! God found that so repulsive that he put him to death as well!

Judah then told Tamar to wait for his youngest son to be old enough to marry her. In the meantime, Judah's wife also died, making him a widower. After Judah recovered from grieving, he went to visit some men shearing sheep, and by the road he saw a prostitute and decided to sleep with her, not realizing, it was actually his daughter-in-law! Tamar was afraid that Judah's youngest son would not be given to her in marriage, and so in a desperate attempt to carry on the family line, she disguised herself and seduced Judah. Eventually, Judah found out she was pregnant, and in a rage of self-righteous anger, demanded she should be put to death. However, with convincing evidence, Tamar revealed that she was impregnated by Judah! She ends up having twins, one whom she names Perez and the other Zerah. And that brings us back to where we started, because Achan is a direct descendent of Zerah! (Genesis 38:1-27).

What is the point of that? The point of that is this family line is extremely messed up! This is not exactly a model family of integrity, character, and godliness! They had a history full of bringing shame and disgrace upon their names and all of Israel.

But here is how I believe this all ties together when it comes to God's promise to redeem. When the Messiah is born, what tribe is he from? If you said, the line of Judah you would be correct! Jesus forever becomes associated with the name of Judah, so much so, that in a vision John the apostle has in Revelation 5, he sees that no one is worthy in the history of humanity and begins to weep. But then, John is told the following, *Do not weep! See, the Lion of the tribe of Judah, the Root of David, has triumphed. He is able to open the scroll and its seven seals* (Revelation 5:5).

Of all the names or tribes Jesus could have associated himself with, he chooses a tribe whose name was associated with shame and disgrace. A family that would seem hopeless and an utter mess. A family maybe least deserving of grace. And that is the very point.

Jesus has gone to all our Valleys of Achor through his death on the cross. The cross itself was a symbol of shame, humiliation, hopelessness, suffering, and death. But Jesus has transformed the cross into a symbol of hope and healing. At the cross, where the Lion of the tribe of Judah was slaughtered, we find transformation and redemption. We find a new identity. We find peace with God. We find hope.

There are solutions for all of us

Your situation is not beyond hope. Your mess is not too messy for Jesus. Your sin is not too great for his grace. Your family drama or shame is not beyond redemption. Do not cut yourself off from the hope found in Jesus Christ, because he has not cut you off! Instead, he calls us in to that hope.

> Of all the names or tribes Jesus could have associated himself with, he chooses a tribe whose name was associated with shame and disgrace. A family that would seem hopeless and an utter mess.

As we conclude this chapter, Lars and I want to simply state that we have had our own battles with despair, depression, loss of hope, and whispers of the enemy to varying degrees in different situations. He is a thief who comes to steal, kill, and destroy as Jesus said in John 10:10. But, Jesus has come for the exact opposite purpose and to counteract the enemy's plans. He has come that we might have life, and life to the fullest. He has come that we may flourish together. He has come to remove our shame and transform our Valleys of Achor into gateways of hope where we, and others, can find new hope. In the worst valleys and deepest pits of despair, God can and does bring transformation that can serve to bring hope to a world in need.

8

The Book Full of Hope

For everything that was written in the past was written to teach us, so that through the endurance taught in the Scriptures and the encouragement they provide we might have hope.
—Romans 15:4

The Bible is the most sold as well as the most widely distributed book in the world. By the end of 2017, the entire Bible had been printed in 670 languages. A further 1517 languages have a complete New Testament, and there are additional compilations in 1,137 languages where at least some portion of the Bible has been translated and distributed.[1]

The word *Bible* comes from *biblia* in Latin and *biblos* in Greek. It means a book, or a series of books. The Bible has also been called the Holy Scriptures, Holy Writ, Scripture, or the Scriptures—all titles that mean sacred writings. The Bible is a compilation of 66 books and letters written by more than 40 authors during a period of approximately 1,500 years. God used their skills, gifts, and different communication styles to give us the Bible. While they addressed their subjects from different vantage points and through various literature styles, their message remains the same in a remarkable way: God is alive and he cares for us so much that he provided a Redeemer in order that we can have fellowship with God forever.

There were only three original languages in which the Bible was written. Most of the Old Testament was written in Hebrew, except for a small percentage in Aramaic. The entire New Testament was written in common Greek, often called Koine Greek.

The Word of God—the Bible—has incredible power to provide hope

One day in the early 1990s, I met the vice mayor of what was then the city of Leningrad in the Soviet Union, and he told me, "I am an atheist. But the books you are giving the students in our schools have such an incredible power that after three months, I have already seen a behavioral change in them." What book was that? It was a portion of the Bible.

A Muslim student in Asia sat down with me some years ago and gently shared, "I am a Muslim. But through this book, I have found a love that is changing my life." *What book was that?* It was the Bible.

In Sweden a young atheist woman who hated the God she did not believe existed, started to read a book a friend had given her in high school. As she read through the pages, she was confronted with the story of the man in the book and it changed her life. *What book was that?* It was the Bible.

There is incredible power in the Bible, the Word of God. The book of Hebrews expresses it like this: *For the word of God is alive and powerful. It is sharper than the sharpest two-edged sword, cutting between soul and spirit, between joint and marrow. It exposes our innermost thoughts and desires* (Hebrews 4:12, NLT).

There is incredible power in the Bible, the Word of God.

Why is this book so special?

Looking at an average Bible, you will notice that it has mostly black ink and thin pages. It's typically covered in black faux leather and is as heavy as a brick! What makes it so special?

In many parts of the Western world, it still has legal usage. For example, in many courts a witness swears to "tell the truth and nothing but the truth," holding his or her hand on the Bible. When the Queen of England was crowned in 1953 the coronation pledge was made with her hand on a Bible.

The legal system in several countries originates from the Old Testament law, while the disciplines of art, music, and literature draw heavily from the imagery found in the pages of this sacred book. But most of all, the Word of God is special because it has the power to transform ordinary lives!

If you were stranded on a desert island and could only have one book with you, which book would you choose? Maybe a *Guide to Building Ships* to help you to get home. You don't want a book that can entertain you. You don't want a self-help book to improve your personality. You want a book that will show you how to get off the island. Today we are trapped on an island called earth, and eventually our stay on this island leads to death unless we are rescued. It's the most hopeless situation we can find ourselves in. We are stranded here, but there is one book that can tell us how to get home to another world, another great future rather than death. The Bible is that book of hope.

The Bible tells us about God

People often hunger for relevance and revelation, wanting to interact with some spiritual being. That is why we have so many different religions in the world. People are searching for God, but by searching for him, we will not find God. He has already revealed himself, and he is actually seeking for us.

Deep in our hearts, we hunger to know him. The Bible tells us that God lives and cares; it tells he is good. We can know him, and our lives can be rescued now. It's in the Bible we discover that

God loves us so much that he became a man in the form of Jesus Christ and came to earth to save us.

Through the Word of God, we have the only guarantee ever offered for life after death, i.e. that you and I simply place our beliefs and trust in Jesus Christ as the one through whom we can find the way, the truth, and the life.

Through the Bible we can be spiritually transformed

The Bible tells us that *all Scripture is inspired by God and is useful to teach us what is true and to make us realize what is wrong in our lives. It corrects us when we are wrong and teaches us to do what is right. God uses it to prepare and equip his people to do every good work* (2 Timothy 3:16-17, NLT).

Whom do you look to for authority in your life? In our country, well-known media personalities often become role models for authority. In the life of a teenager, parents or teachers often become authority figures. For those working, their bosses can be an important factor in their lives. In church, it may be the pastor who tells you what to do, based on the tradition of the church.

However, the Word of God, the Bible, needs to be our infallible guide. Have you placed yourself under the authority of the Bible? This entire book is inspired by God. You must decide under what you are going to place the ultimate authority in your life.

At one point in my life, I had to make that decision. Should I believe the godless philosophies being taught in my nation of Sweden? Should I accept the disbelief I found in some of the liberal churches around me, that questioned the historicity of Jesus, as well as his death and resurrection? Or should I put my faith in the Bible and its life-changing message? One day at the Bible college I attended in London, I bowed down by my bed and prayed, "Lord, I submit my life and will to the teaching of your Word, whatever the cost and whatever may happen."

The purpose of the Word of God in our lives

You were just told in the earlier verse that *God uses it to prepare and equip his people to do every good work.* This does not just mean on the weekend when you go to church. It means that you become a transformed person who wants to live for Jesus Christ and do his work every day of the week, every day of the year. If Jesus Christ, the living Word, and the Bible—God's written Word—are allowed to do their work in your mind, heart, and will, then you can be so transformed that good things are the result in your life. Every day you will say, "Here is my opportunity to live out the kingdom of God."

Sometimes we believe that if we know enough Scripture by heart and if we have enough theological knowledge, everything will be fine. We think knowing a lot about theology means spiritual authority. We can outline every book in the Bible; we can quote every verse and criticize those who cannot. But remember, it's the Scriptures that point to Jesus. It's not how much we know about the Bible that is important, but how we are transformed by what we know.

Remember the Pharisees? Jesus had to say to them, *You study the Scriptures diligently because you think that in them you have eternal life. These are the very Scriptures that testify about me* (John 5:39).

The Word of God speaks to us many different ways

In his book *Primal*, Mark Batterson expresses it in this way:

> According to rabbinic tradition, every word of sacred Scripture has seventy faces and six hundred thousand meanings.[2]
>
> If I had to describe Scripture in a single word, it would be *kaleidoscopic*. You can read the same verse on different occasions and it will speak to you in totally different ways. It reminds me of the adage attributed to the Greek philosopher Heraclitus: "You never step into the same river twice." In a

similar vein, you never read the same verse of Scripture the same way twice. And that is a testament to the divine Author. The Spirit who inspired the writers of Scripture thousands of years ago is the same Spirit who illuminates readers today. And his illumination of Scripture is based on his intimate and infinite knowledge of your personality, your circumstances, your dreams, your doubts, your history, and your destiny. That is why Scripture speaks to us in such kaleidoscopic ways.[3]

What else do we find in the Bible?

Sooner or later, all people in the world wrestle with some basic questions in life. In the Bible, we find the answers to all these questions: Who am I? And whom can I become to make a difference? What gifts have I been endowed with? Why am I here?

> It's not how much we know about the Bible that is important, but how we are transformed by what we know.

What is the purpose of life? Who are the people around me? For example, why was I born in Kentucky and not in India? What will I leave behind? Not so much in material resources, but as a legacy and impact, and finally one of the key questions of life: What happens when I die?

The answers to these questions in the Word of God will transform us and make us the people we were created to be.

This book will give you promises, which, as they come true, will enrich your lives beyond what you can imagine. The words of this book will guide us through some of the most important decisions in our lives. Through its pages we will receive comfort when we have been hurt, disappointed, lost all hope, and are without direction. The book will both encourage us and give us a new view of the future.

What does the Bible say about itself?

God's Word is a mirror

> *Those who hear and don't act are like those who glance in the mirror, walk away, and two minutes later have no idea who they are, what they look like. But whoever catches a glimpse of the revealed counsel of God—the free life!—even out of the corner of his eye, and sticks with it, is no distracted scatterbrain but a man or woman of action. That person will find delight and affirmation in the action.* (James 1:23-25, MSG)

It's God's Holy Spirit who convicts us of the wrongs in our lives. That is what the Bible calls *sin*. You and I cannot come to God unless we are convicted by the Holy Spirit, and he often uses the Word to do so. When we are willing to admit that we are sinners, we are being affected through the work of the Holy Spirit. The Bible always points to Jesus. He says, *These are written that you may believe that Jesus is the Messiah, the Son of God* (John 20:31 NLT).

It's through faith in Jesus that you find eternal life. If we wait until we can understand it all intellectually, we will never find him. We will be lost.

The university professor needs to come by faith to Jesus Christ. The businessperson has to come by faith. The housewife needs to come by faith. The student needs to come by faith. When we come and look at him in that mirror—the Word of God—he stretches his arms out to us to forgive us of our sin, cleanse us, and reshape us into new people.

God's Word is food for the soul

I love to eat. Most of all, I like ice cream. Eating two scoops tastes delicious, but if I eat 25 scoops at the same time I would get very sick.

It's just the opposite with the Word of God. The more we eat, the more we want, and the less we eat, the less hungry we get. *Like newborn babies, crave pure spiritual milk, so that by it you may grow up in your salvation* (1 Peter 2:2). *But solid food is for the mature, who by constant use have trained themselves to distinguish good from evil* (Hebrews 5:14).

God's Word is a light

We live in a dark world and often it feels so dark inside. But the light from the tiniest match will make the darkness flee from any room. God's Word is such a light in our lives. *Your word is a lamp for my feet, and a light on my path* (Psalm 119:105).

God's Word is like a knife

When the Scriptures speak about God's Word being a knife, it isn't suggesting that God wants to murder us. But the Word of God penetrates our inner lives and provides the change we so desperately need.

An industrialist sat in his office and contemplated on the biggest business deal of his life. But in doing so, he would have to break some basic ethical laws. He opened the Bible on his office desk and began to read. Suddenly he decided: There will be no deal.

There was a woman who had an affair with a man. The following day she was going to tell her husband that she was ready to visit the lawyer to file for divorce. Sleep did not come easily that night, as memories from Sunday school long ago flashed through her mind. "People reap what they sow," echoed through her head as she tossed and turned in her bed. It had been a long time since she had read the book, but suddenly she remembered its teachings: Purity, responsibility, faithfulness, and love. She confessed her sin to God through the night and asked for forgiveness. In the morning she sent the other man an e-mail and told him: Forget me! It's over!

A young girl was wrestling with the calling to serve the Lord in full-time service. She had been offered a tempting top job with a good salary. She read Luke 9 about not turning back after having put her hand to the plow. Suddenly she fell to her knees and prayed, "Lord here am I! Send me!"

For the word of God is alive and powerful. It is sharper than the sharpest two-edged sword, cutting between soul and spirit, between joint and marrow. It exposes our innermost thoughts and desires (Hebrews 4:12, NLT).

God's Word is a shield

We often feel attacked in our emotions or in our feeble faith. We sense temptation lurking where we least expect it. God's Word shields us against doubt, guilt, insecurity, or giving in to temptation. *You are my refuge and my shield* (Psalm 119:114, NLT).

God's Word is a map

Once I was driving with the map on my steering wheel. I was late for a church service and in a hurry. As I turned right, there was no church where it was supposed to be. Suddenly I realized I was holding the map upside down and was far from where I needed to be. God's Word is like a map for our lives. It's not just enough to read it, but we must also follow its instructions. *Direct my footsteps according to your word* (Psalm 119:133).

The Word of God in our lives

The Bible is the inspired Word of God. *All Scripture is inspired by God and is useful to teach us what is true and to make us realize what is wrong in our lives. It corrects us when we are wrong and teaches us to do what is right* (2 Timothy 3:16, NLT).

Primarily, the Bible tells the story of the Creator God and his love for the human race. We learn of his purposes and plans from the beginning of time until now. We discover that he wants to

> It's not just enough to read it, but we must also follow its instructions.

have a personal relationship with us as human beings. The central theme of the Bible is God's plan to bring us salvation. In the Old Testament, the concept of salvation is best described in Israel's deliverance from Egypt as recorded in Exodus, the second book of the Bible.

The New Testament describes how salvation comes to us through Jesus Christ. *For God so loved the world that he gave his one and only Son, that whoever believes in him shall not perish but have eternal life* (John 3:16). By faith in Jesus, people are brought into an abundant life here on earth and for eternity.

It's in the Bible that God reveals himself to us. We discover his nature and character, his love, his justice, his forgiveness, and his truth. Many have called the Bible a handbook for life. *Your word is a lamp for my feet, a light on my path* (Psalm 119:105).

The Bible is an extraordinary book; it's diverse in its content and literary styles and is written by a large group of authors. It reveals God's plan and will for your life.

For many years, the Bible was a forbidden book, available only to clergy and scholars. Today it's the inspiration of life for approximately one third of the world's population.

Biblical illiteracy

A few years ago a very popular TV show host asked his audience some direct questions from the Bible. "Name one of the Ten Commandments," he said.

Someone answered, "God helps those who help themselves." This quote is not even in the Bible!

"Name one of the apostles!" the host continued. Not one person in the audience knew the answer. "Name the four men in the Beatles group!" the host asked.

"George, Paul, John, and Ringo," answered the audience with one voice.

In a recent Gallup poll only 2 out of 10 could name who preached the Sermon on the Mount. Some thought it was Billy Graham. Twelve percent of Christians think that Noah's wife was called Joan of Arc. At the same time, 75 percent of Americans say they believe the Bible is either the Word of God or inspired by God.[4] So if this is God's book, why don't we care to read it?

Tyndale House Publishers did a survey on this subject and found that 64 percent of survey respondents didn't read the Bible because of the busyness of their lives.[5]

While Christians may be able to recognize major figures in the Bible such as Adam, Abraham, David, Solomon, Jesus, and Paul, most of them are not able to put these biblical figures in chronological order. Why is that?

In my younger days, when I worked with Youth for Christ in Britain, we conducted Bible quizzes. Teenagers memorized an enormous number of Bible verses that they could rattle off by heart. However, it seemed that the words of those passages seldom went from the memory banks of their brains to their hearts. Now the pendulum has swung to the opposite side, where people cannot have the Word touch their hearts, because they've never even read it, let alone committed it to memory.

Americans used to be a Bible reading society. When I first moved to the United States in 1978, it was said that 79 percent of the population read the Bible at least once a month. Today only 16 percent of Christians say they read the Bible every day.[6] In one US mega church, 32 percent don't read the Bible at all, while 68 percent have read something in the last year. Less than 25 percent of regular churchgoers have ever read through the entire Bible.

Research has shown that among regular churchgoers in Britain, 16 percent (same percentage as in the United States) read the Bible every day. The director of Churches in Mission for the Evangelical Alliance in Britain says: "We own more Bibles than we will ever use, but we are slowly starving to death because we have lost our appetite for Scripture."[7]

> In one US mega church, 32 percent don't read the Bible at all, while 68 percent have read something in the last year. Less than 25 percent of regular churchgoers have ever read through the entire Bible.

A fairly recent survey, among people with a median age of 34 years, in a progressive, seeker-sensitive, exploding Colorado church, revealed that more than 25 percent of regular attendees never read their Bibles and two thirds of regular attendees could recall less than 10 Bible verses from memory.[8]

The change needs to come—not just in memorizing Scripture but understanding how it hangs together. More than Sunday school classes, every church needs a program that introduces the Bible as the "handbook for life."

The failure is not because people cannot read. They simply choose not to. That the Bible is confusing and hard to understand is an invalid excuse when modern Bible translations and paraphrases make biblical concepts extremely clear.

It has such influence

For more than 70 years, the Bible was a forbidden book in the former Soviet Union. If you owned a copy, you could end up in jail. When the Iron Curtain fell in 1989, one of the most sought-after possessions was a Bible.[9] A few years later I received this letter from a Russian woman: "I heard from my grandmother that there was a book called the Bible, but I never saw one in my life—until now! I got a copy and I read it over and over again and I cannot see the end of what I will get out of it."

This woman had realized the value of the Bible in her life. There is not a problem in the world that this book cannot deal with, whether on a national or personal scale. So what should you do with it?

Using this book will increase your hope

I used to train young people and more mature Christians as well as pastors about getting into the Word using my five fingers as an illustration. One point per finger, I would count down: read it, study it, memorize it, meditate on it, and obey it. Here is an in-depth look at each of these interactions with the Word of God.

Read it

Begin to read it every day. Don't necessarily start from the beginning because you may be bogged down after a few days. This is what I do: I read a chapter from the Old Testament historical books, such as the first five books or 1 and 2 Samuel, 1 and 2 Kings, 1 and 2 Chronicles, or Ezra and Nehemiah; one chapter from the Prophets (like Isaiah, Amos, or Obadiah), one chapter from Psalms or Proverbs; one chapter from one of the Gospels or Acts and one chapter from the letters in the New Testament. It doesn't take any longer than reading the newspaper, which is filled with bad news. As you sample different parts of the Bible each day, you will give good news equal time!

Study it

This is more than just casual reading. Take up a theme, like "salvation" or "holiness" and look up every reference you can find. Or study the life of Abraham, David, Esther, or Paul. Use a concordance and study any subject in depth. You will find out how rich the Word of God is.

Memorize it

You may think you have a bad memory. But do you remember your birth date? Your shoe and shirt size? Your vital signs? Your address? Your cell phone number? There is nothing wrong with your memory! It's fine!

I have hidden your word in my heart! said the psalmist. How can we do that if we have not memorized it? There are many simple Bible memorization programs. Use a modern translation so what you learn by heart makes sense to you.

Meditate on it

This is different from Eastern meditation. Psalm 1 says, *You thrill to God's Word, you chew on Scripture day and night* (Psalm 1:2, MSG). Just like a cow chews the cud, you concentrate on a passage of Scripture for a while and chew it over. Perhaps you read it in the morning. You memorize it; you pray over it; you say it out loud and pray throughout the day, "Holy Spirit, tell me how I can apply this verse from the Word to my life today."

Obey it

As biblical truth becomes a reality for you, you need to do one major thing: obey what you have read and apply it to your daily life.

Don't just go through the Word, but let the Word go through you, and shape you into his image. Don't just count on your own willpower but ask him for the power to do what you hear his Spirit telling you to do.

What are you "eating" today? Ten percent newspapers and magazines, 50 percent video content, 15 percent radio, 25 percent novels and other books and 0 percent Bible? No wonder you are unaware of your spiritual appetite.

Begin to eat. The more you eat the hungrier you will become—and you will grow healthy and mature spiritually.

9

Hope in Our Old Age

Against all hope, Abraham in hope believed and so became the
father of many nations, just as it had been said to him, "So
shall your offspring be."
—Romans 4:18

In this chapter and the next I (Ben) want to address two insidious lies I believe the enemy of our souls uses quite effectively to sideline many people when it comes to kingdom usefulness and productive service. The first is the lie that we are too old to be significantly used by God anymore.

In certain cultures of the world, elderly people are something to be revered, honored, respected, and sought out for wisdom. For example, in China, students continue meeting with their teachers long after graduating to show their respect.

Unfortunately in other cultures such as in the United States, there is a sense of "pushing aside" the elderly and a dread of aging. We've even built a whole culture around working hard to retire early. While retirement, or changing of roles in life, is not necessarily the problem, retiring from service to God absolutely is! Why throw away a lifetime of experience, lessons learned, and wisdom gained? Why believe your best days are behind you instead of ahead of you? You now have more to invest in others than ever before and can be available to God in new ways you weren't before. In other words, why do we focus on all we can't do, instead of what we can do? Better yet, what can God do through us after years of working in us?

God can use the wisdom you have gained over the years

My friend, Daniel Grothe, a pastor at New Life Church in Colorado Springs, writes the following encouragement in his book *Chasing Wisdom*:

> The experiences and the perspectives you have gained are something money can't buy and youth can't replicate. It just takes *time* to grow old and to see what you have seen. You stand on the precipice of realizing your greatest potential. Yet the society in which we live seems to be actively telling you either that you're not needed anymore or that you should retreat into leisure (to golf or go on a vacation), away from the life you once lived. Yes, you should enjoy these years, but your contribution shouldn't come to an end. In fact, this is your moment to bear the most fruit you've ever borne. This is the season where God intends to multiply your reach and extend the wisdom and experiences you have gained.[1]

Think about some of the great saints of the Bible. Many of them were used most significantly in their later years for what we most remember them for. For example, Moses was 80 years old when he received the call from God to lead his people out of slavery in Egypt, after 40 years growing up in Egypt and 40 years as a shepherd! (Deuteronomy 34:7). Noah was more than 500 years old when he began building the ark and was 600 years old when the flood took place (Genesis 7:6). Talk about old . . . he was anciently old! When an angel tells Zechariah that he and his wife are going to have a baby (John the Baptizer), he specifically notes his disbelief because of their old age (Luke 1:18). Luke chapter 2 records when the baby Jesus was dedicated in the temple, a man named Simeon spoke prophetic words over Jesus. It's noted twice that Simeon was old. God had promised him that events surrounding the Messiah would happen before Simeon died, and when Simeon held the baby Jesus in his arms he says, *Sovereign Lord, as you have promised, you may now dismiss your servant in peace* (Luke 2:29). Immediately following this encounter, another prophet, a widow named Anna, enters the scene and she speaks words about Jesus to onlookers. Again, we are told specifically that *she was very old* (Luke 2:36).

I could go on with other notable characters in the Bible, but hopefully you see even from these examples, that some of God's greatest works and fulfillment of his promises to his people occurred in people's old age. This tells us that God can work in any stage of our lives. Age is not something that prevents him from working in special and significant ways. There is hope for us all no matter our age!

> **God can work in any stage of our lives. Age is not something that prevents him from working in special and significant ways! There is hope for us all no matter our age!**

We can still learn lessons from Abraham and Sarah

The biblical example I want to draw attention to most is that of Abraham and Sarah. Let's take a look at the entire passage about them in Romans 4:

> *Against all hope, Abraham in hope believed and so became the father of many nations, just as it had been said to him, "So shall your offspring be." Without weakening in his faith, he faced the fact that his body was as good as dead—since he was about a hundred years old—and that Sarah's womb was also dead. Yet he did not waver through unbelief regarding the promise of God, but was strengthened in his faith and gave glory to God, being fully persuaded that God had power to do*

> *what he had promised. This is why "it was credited to him as*
> *righteousness." The words "it was credited to him" were written*
> *not for him alone, but also for us, to whom God will credit*
> *righteousness—for us who believe in him who raised Jesus our*
> *Lord from the dead.* (vv. 18-24)

Note the utter lack of realistic human hope in that particular situation. *Against all hope* is the way it begins. The reason there was no human hope in this situation, was precisely because of Abraham's old age and Sarah's barren womb. God had promised to make Abraham *the father of many nations.* But now he was *about a hundred years old* and *Sarah's womb was also dead.* Not only was her womb "dead," but humanly speaking, so was this promise God gave them.

But despite the lack of human hope (based on normal human conditions), this passage tells us that *Abraham in hope believed.* Now, it's important to note before we go further, that Abraham was not in denial about his circumstances, age, or human limitations. We are told, *He faced the fact that his body was as good as dead . . . and that Sarah's womb was also dead.* In other words, he looked at his condition, his wife's condition—their bodily limitations in their old age,—and faced those realities head on. Certain teachers in certain circles have taught in recent years that you should not "accept" or "declare" any "negative" realities. But this is not the biblical example. Abraham was not in denial. But he also was not placing his hope in only human possibilities or abilities. He had already learned the hard way that when we try to take matters into our hands and bring about God's promises in our own strength according to our own abilities, it breeds disastrous results (Genesis 16). Plus, now he was in a position where that was not even a viable option. His only hope was to place his hope in God, who is not limited by our limitations and for whom nothing is impossible!

In fact, despite acknowledging the reality of his circumstances, *he did not waver through unbelief regarding the promise of God, but was strengthened in his faith and gave glory to God, being fully persuaded that God had power to do what he had promised.* Abraham's hope was not dashed by his old age or circumstances but was empowered by his faith in God and his promise to him! Abraham was not relying on himself, but fully on the ability and power of God to perform what he had promised in his life!

And that very promise, for which we most remember Abraham, happened toward the end of his life, not his younger years or prime of life! God is not done with you yet either! He may be saving his most significant work in you and through you for your later part of life!

Right before this promise was fulfilled to Abraham, God appeared to him to reaffirm this promise and relationship with Abraham. Genesis 17:1-9 records this story in detail. It begins by noting that *when Abram was ninety-nine years old, the LORD appeared to him and said, "I am God Almighty; walk before me faithfully and be blameless. Then I will make my covenant between me and you and will greatly increase your numbers."*

What's special about this is that God had already appeared, made, and confirmed this promise to Abraham several times before in his life. You may have already had some significant moments in the presence of God in your life and had him reveal awesome promises to you in his Word. But God delights in keeping relationship with us fresh, renewing his relationship with us and reminding us of his promises, no matter how old we are or how many experiences we may have already had.

When Abram is 99 years old, his name is officially changed to Abraham. Genesis 17:5 records God declaring, *No longer will you be called Abram; your name will be Abraham, for I have made you a father of many nations.* A change of name signifies a change of character. It took 99 years for the deep work of inward transformation to really take hold in changing the core of Abraham's identity! Character takes time. And character, like fine wine, should become better over time and with age. That is not always the case, however, when it comes to character. Sometimes the older we become the crankier we seem to get, or more we let down our guard and start to think we can compromise more in our attitude, actions, words, and treatment of others. Ed Stetzer, in his book *Christians in the Age of Outrage*, writes, "One of the biggest obstacles to seriously engaging the message of Jesus is the character and conduct of its messengers. We must acknowledge that the watching world does not sense that we are engaging them with a winsome love."[2]

God intends for us to become more Christ-like the older we get. In fact, Christ-likeness is God's very purpose for our lives as believers. Many people know the promise in Romans 8:28 that says, *And we know that in all things God works for the good of those who love him, who have been called according to his purpose.* What a wonderful promise this is! But this is a conditional promise. It's conditioned on those who *love God* and *have been called according to his purpose.* Have you ever asked what God's purpose is to which we have been called? Verse 9 answers that question, although in some pretty loaded theological terms that might seem intimidating at first, *For those God foreknew he also predestined to be conformed to the image of his Son, that he might be the firstborn among many brothers and sisters.* Simply put, God's purpose for my life and your life and every believer's life is one and the same: for us to become like Christ! In other words, every circumstance, event, relationship, and role in life is meant to facilitate that very purpose. But some of the deepest inward transformation of character and coming into our true identity in Christ occurs later in life, having been formed and fashioned by many trials, challenges, and experiences.

God goes on to tell Abraham this in Genesis 17:6, *I will make you very fruitful; I will make nations of you, and kings will come from you.* Again, it's in his old age when God affirms that Abraham will be "fruitful." True fruitfulness does not happen

> **God's purpose for my life and your life and every believer is one and the same: for us to become like Christ!**

overnight either, much like character. Fruitfulness can take years of plowing, sowing, watering, and waiting. This is an important principle for our "everything now" culture! Character can't be forced and neither can fruitfulness. Our role is faithfulness. God's job is to make us fruitful.

Further, in Genesis 17:7-8, God says this to Abraham:

> *I will establish my covenant as an everlasting covenant between me and you and your descendants after you for the generations to come, to be your God and the God of your descendants after you. The whole land of Canaan, where you now reside as a foreigner, I will give as an everlasting possession to you and your descendants after you; and I will be their God.*

What is happening here? The answer is God is "establishing" Abraham and bringing Abraham into the fullness of what he has promised him as his inheritance. Abraham has been wandering around the Promised Land for years but as more of an outsider than a true insider. But now, God is securing not only his future but also his legacy that will continue through his descendants. In fact, this portion concludes with God saying to Abraham, *As for you, you must keep my covenant, you and your descendants after you for the generations to come* (v. 9). Old age is not the time to relax in our relationship with God; it's the time to renew our relationship with God as he brings all his promises to pass in our lives and for future generations!

We are never too old

This all reminds us there is tremendous hope in our old age. We are never too old for God to work in special and significant ways! Let me close this chapter with a few meaningful stories of how I have seen this reality at work around the world in my travels with *ServeNow*.

I will never forget a 100-year-old woman in a village in Nepal, who interrupted me while I was speaking to the crowd prior to giving out blankets. In this village, and many like this one, people can't afford even a warm blanket. In the winter, temperatures drop to freezing, and many have no heat. As a result, many die or become sick, especially children and elderly people. In fact, one year we visited a village where a couple of hundred children walked barefoot five hours down a mountain to meet us where the road ends. They did all that in order to receive a knitted hat, a fleece jacket and warm pants. The local government official told us that in the winter these children dig holes in the ground just to try to keep themselves shielded from the cold wind in the mountains. It was heartbreaking but very meaningful to be able to provide warm winter clothes to these young people who trekked another five hours back up the mountain to where they lived!

Anyway, back to the 100-year-old woman who interrupted me. So, there I was addressing the crowd, trying to tell them that when we wrap these blankets around them and give them as a free gift, it was meant to be a picture of God's love for them and his free gift of eternal life in Christ Jesus. However, this woman kept trying to talk to me as I spoke. I wasn't sure what was happening or if something might be wrong. However, when one of our Nepali translators began telling me what she was saying, I realized

I could stop preaching, because she had already got the message! She was so excited about the blanket that she was saying thank you over and over again. She said, "You are like angels that have come down from heaven to show us God's love! You are all like sons to me!"

Just imagine that. One hundred years old and a blanket being given to her was one of the most meaningful moments of her long life.

Another time I was leading a mission trip team to Ukraine. On one of the days, we visited people to whom *ServeNow* had provided wheelchairs. Many disabled people in Ukraine can't afford a wheelchair and live their whole lives without one. That's why one of the projects over the years has been to send 40-foot containers filled with medical equipment and wheelchairs for underequipped hospitals and disabled people.

One of the people we visited on that trip was an older gentleman named Peter. When Peter was very young, he stepped on a landmine from World War 2 near his home where he still lived years later. It was only recently through *ServeNow* that he received his first wheelchair for outside use! Not only would he be able to get around outside, but his sister, who helps take care of him, told us that now he can help her! It happened to be raining the day when we visited Peter, so we gathered inside where we saw the little handmade, wooden slab scooter he gets around on indoors. As we were leaving, a team member said the family would be in our prayers, and they responded that they would be praying for us so we can help more people.

Our national director in Ukraine shared a great story with us from the *ServeNow* Christmas gift program, where we give out shoeboxes filled with 20 or so different items to disenfranchised families in Ukraine. For many of these people and children, it's the first time anyone had ever given them a Christmas gift. That was true for an elderly woman who in the past had been a fierce communist activist. She was well known for leading rallies and, in her day, was even regularly featured in the media. However, when our team came with a gift for her and shared God's love, she was moved to tears and gave her life to Christ! Just a day later, we found out she had died.

You are not too old if you are still alive and reading this!

10

Hope for the Young

Here is a boy with five small barley loaves and two small fish,
but how far will they go among so many?
—John 6:9

One of my absolute favorite stories in the Bible, which I return to in various situations, is the famous story of the multitude that was miraculously fed through a young boy with a few fish and loaves. The richness to this story is so great that it would take another book to fully unpack in and of itself!

For this chapter, I want to use this story as the primary text to make the biblical case that there is hope regardless of our age, whether old as we looked at in the previous chapter or young, as we will examine in this chapter.

Before we dive into this story, however, let me point out a few other notable examples and passages in Scripture where God used young people in significant ways. Let me start with a fun one. Do you know the age of the youngest King of Israel? Second Chronicles 24:1 tells us, *Joash was seven years old when he became king, and he reigned in Jerusalem forty years.* Seven years old! Can you imagine? But it's important to note that Joash is commented on as being one of the good kings who, *did what was right in the eyes of the LORD* (2 Chronicles 24:2). Other notable examples would include David when he defeated Goliath (possibly around

17 years old).[1] Daniel, Shadrach, Meshach, and Abednego, were probably teenagers when they were taken captive to Babylon, and yet they rose to great prominence, even in their youth. They defied worshiping the image the king had set up and commanded them to bow down to it under threat of death. Mary, the mother of Jesus, was probably in her very early teens, and Joseph only slightly older. Jesus' disciples were probably in the 20s to early 30s when Jesus called them, and even he was only 30 when his public ministry began.

God chose to use a young slave girl

Another story of God using a young girl is found in 2 Kings 5. One of the great army commanders of the time, a man named Naaman, is called a *valiant soldier* but then we are informed *he had leprosy* (v. 1). Leprosy at the time, even as it still is in some cultures, was a social stigma that would have been highly embarrassing to Naaman. But in 2 Kings 5:2 we are told that one day, bands of raiders from Aram had gone out and had taken captive a young girl from Israel, and she served Naaman's wife.

> Jesus' disciples were probably in the 20s to early 30s when Jesus called them, and even he was only 30 when his public ministry began.

In today's world, child labor, along with human trafficking, is a massive global issue. At *ServeNow*, we have some fantastic skill-training programs to protect those at risk and establish dignity in the lives of those who want to learn a marketable trade. But over the years, we have heard and seen some truly horrifying and tragic stories involving trafficking and child labor.

I mention this because here is a young girl who is forcibly removed from her home and family and forced to work for the commanding officer's wife. If anyone would have had reason to be bitter and without hope, it would have been this young girl. However, when she finds out that her mistress's husband has leprosy, her comment is one of genuine concern and compassion. She said to her mistress, *If only my master would see the prophet who is in Samaria! He would cure him of his leprosy* (v. 3). As a result of her statement, Naaman does go to see this prophet Elijah and does receive healing from his leprosy in a way that he becomes a worshiper of the God of Israel!

This girl could have kept that information to herself. She did not have to reveal this insight. But she demonstrates a childlike tenderness of heart, despite what she had been through, toward her "enemy." Now, maybe Naaman and his wife treated her well, but the fact remains, her childlike faith and hope serve as a great example for us today. And that is what the faith of a child is meant to teach the rest of us who so easily grow more and more cynical, and sometimes even bitter with age and experience.

Little can be much in God's hand

When I was a teenager, I did some babysitting for friends of my parents. One of the families had three boys. All three were perfectly healthy. However, one day, not while I was babysitting, the youngest fell and hit the side of his head in such a way that it ended up causing lasting brain damage among other physical problems. He almost died, but it altered his life and, of course, the life of every family member. Fast-forward 17 years later. He recently graduated from high school and is a young man. When I joined *ServeNow*, I was invited to speak at a group he is a part of at a church called the A-Team. The A-Team is a group of young people with various disabilities and challenges. As I prayed about what to share with them about *ServeNow*, I decided to share about how they could collect spare change in jars. Once a year, they could then take those coins to the bank and every $15 worth would provide warm clothes for other children and young people, as well as elderly people in remote villages in the Himalayan mountains.

This young man, Mark, became super excited about it to the point that he started collecting so much spare change that he went and found a bigger jar than the ones we were giving out as a ministry! Every time I would see him or visit my parents' house there would be another jar full of coins from Mark! But what touched me most about this is Mark's joy and hope of making a real difference in other people's lives. And that brings me to the main story in Scripture for this chapter from John 6 and the young boy whose few fish and loaves fed more than 5,000 people.

> When Jesus looked up and saw a great crowd coming toward him, he said to Philip, "Where shall we buy bread for these people to eat?" He asked this only to test him, for he already had in mind what he was going to do.
> Philip answered him, "It would take more than half a year's wages to buy enough bread for each one to have a bite!"
> Another of his disciples, Andrew, Simon Peter's brother, spoke up, "Here is a boy with five small barley loaves and two small fish, but how far will they go among so many?" (John 6:5-9)

Have you ever asked yourself why Jesus turned to his disciples—specifically Philip—and asked them, *Where shall we buy bread for these people to eat?* (v. 5) The next verse even goes on to tell us that *He asked this only to test him, for he already had in mind what he was going to do.* If Jesus already knew what he was going to do, why did he ask this to test his disciples and cause them to stress out about the finances and practicality about it? Also, why didn't Jesus just handle this miracle entirely himself, creating something out of nothing?

This story teaches us that Jesus doesn't shy away from putting us in situations that stretch our faith and produce stomach ulcers!

He does this, however, not to stress us out, but to draw us in as participants in the unfolding of his miracles! As Mark Batterson thoughtfully has put it in his book *The Grave Robber:*

> Everyone wants a miracle. But here's the catch: no one wants to be in a situation that necessitates one! Of course, you can't have one without the other.
>
> The prerequisite for a miracle is a problem, and the bigger the problem, the greater the potential miracle.[2]

God loves to include us in his miracles

For some reason, God loves to include us in the outworking of his miracles. I absolutely love this about him and his hand in *ServeNow*. Week in and week out, we receive story after story of lives being touched and transformed because of the generosity of others in giving, praying, going, and partnering.

I have also found myself scratching my head, or more like panicking and stressing out to our finance director, much like Philip does here in response to Jesus' question, *"Where shall we buy bread for these people to eat?"*. . .*Philip answered him, "It would take*

Jesus does not shy away from putting us in situations that stretch our faith and produce stomach ulcers!

more than half a year's wages to buy enough bread for each one to have a bite!" In other words, how in the world are we going to find the funding or income to fulfill that need or this need?

It was at this point that another disciple enters the story. Andrew spoke up, *Here is a boy with five small barley loaves and two small fish, but how far will they go among so many?* This is comical. As soon as the words leave Andrew's mouth, he immediately regrets it and tries to walk it back recognizing the foolishness of what he was saying. Yes, there was some available food, but it was nothing compared to the need in front of them.

I find this comical because I find myself in this position quite often. I wonder in disbelief how we will secure funding for various needs, especially in comparison to what we have available. Yet, over and over again, just like in this story, we see God take what little we have, bless it, multiply it, and use it to fulfill more than we think is possible! I love how Jesus does not dismiss what this young boy has available and is offering, but to encourage it, take it, give thanks for it, break it, distribute it, and, along the way, multiply it to be more than what was needed by the crowd. They even had leftovers for themselves!

God wants to use what you have

Here is the lesson: we are never too young and never without enough to make a difference even when it seems as if we have little compared to the need in front of us. The key is to simply make ourselves available to Jesus and, with childlike faith, be willing to give to him what we have.

I love how God challenges an aging Moses to deliver his people out of Egypt by asking, *What is that in your hands?* (Exodus 4:2). Moses was wrestling with all kinds of insecurities and excuses and had just asked God, *What if they do not believe me or listen to me and say, "The LORD did not appear to you?"* (Exodus 4:1). God's response was to use what Moses had available in his hands—an ordinary shepherd's staff—to become a miraculous sign for his people. What's in your hands? What might you be overlooking because you're looking for something that isn't so "ordinary?" Why do we even think we have to be something special or have significant wealth or be extraordinarily intelligent to be used by a God who possesses far more power, wisdom, and resources than we could ever imagine? He is not dependent on our "greatness." Rather, he can use our ordinary lives to work in extraordinary ways!

Think of Jesus' first miracle, when he turned water into wine. There again, he didn't start with nothing. He started with what was available even though it was completely ordinary: water. But he transformed it into something special. Even the elements of communion are very ordinary. Yet, the act of communion becomes something very sacred as we honor Jesus and his sacrifice for us.

Think of Jesus' own disciples. They were not the elite or important of the day. They were ordinary, average men. In Acts 4:13, after Peter and John boldly declare the Gospel to the religious leaders, the passage says, *When they saw the courage of Peter and John and realized that they were unschooled, ordinary men, they were astonished and they took note that these men had been with Jesus.* It's being with Jesus that results in his doing something special with our ordinary lives! Giving him what we have and using what's available in childlike faith results in miracles unfolding!

This is the blessing of the youth. They are still naïve enough and foolish enough to attempt impossible things that sometimes the rest of us are too cynical to think will matter! Young age is not a limitation to the Ancient of Days!

A hasty decision leads to long-term blessings

Let me illustrate this with a story from my life. I was just starting college at the time when I went to a worship festival in Pennsylvania called Creation Festival. This event was a big thing at the time, drawing some of the most popular worship bands every year. That year, I heard someone from Compassion International talk about children in other countries needing monthly sponsors. I was moved by the presentation and went to the table and picked out two children to sponsor, a boy and girl, despite having very little money. A few months into sponsoring them, I realized I might have made a mistake and could not afford to sponsor both. Embarrassed, I went to my parents and asked if they would take over sponsoring the girl from Ecuador. Needless to say, they weren't really happy about my irresponsible and irrational "faith," but they graciously took her on.

But then, something unexpected happened. Somewhere along the line, God put it on the hearts of my parents to visit that girl. Up to that point, they had never been on a mission trip out of the country. That trip, however, would end up changing their whole life, and a modest estimation would be to say it also changed thousands upon thousands of other children and people in need. Because, after that trip, my dad decided that if he ended up making any money from a side job he had just started by selling things on eBay, they would give 50 percent to missions. My dad insists that beginning that very week sales tripled and have not stopped yet! His profits were so good he retired early to focus entirely on the eBay business. My parents began sponsoring up to 30 children a month through Compassion International, while also being able to give significantly to others in need, including *ServeNow*. This fulfills a promise I felt God gave me in my youth, that one day our family would serve him together in missions.

Also, I would be lying if I said I didn't also like to remind my parents that none of that would have happened if it wasn't for the "reckless" and "irresponsible" faith and foolish optimism of a college son! So yes, I say without shame, they'd better continue giving generously to the mission organization their son leads!

In all seriousness though, the elder apostle Paul wrote to the young pastor Timothy, *Don't let anyone look down on you because you are young, but set an example for the believers in speech, in conduct, in love, in faith and in purity* (1 Timothy 4:12). I have had to encourage myself with this verse many times over the years. I started preaching and leading various groups and Bible studies when I was 17 years old. I was called to a role as senior pastor of a church when I was 25. I was then approached by our founder of *Serve-*

Now, at the age of 30 to be trained by him for a few years and step into his role as president. Until I reached my mid-30s, I constantly heard people say, "You're so young!" or "You're too young!"

You would not believe the battles I've had with insecurity because of the roles I found myself in at a young age or situations I have had to respond to that were beyond my abilities.

But let me bring our founder, Lars Dunberg, in at this point to share a bit of his story in connection with approaching me to lead *ServeNow* . . .

My experience opens the door for Ben some 40 years later

ServeNow's first president was my daughter Maria Sturt. After the first 15 months, she realized that the leadership responsibility took a too high demand of her time, especially with three teenagers at home, so she asked to be relieved of her role. I was the chair of the board and immediately called an emergency board meeting. After some deliberations I was asked if I would take on the presidency for a period of no more than three years, and with the caveat that the board would find a successor during that time. I certainly agreed to the maximum term of three years but completely refused to give the board the right to find my successor. "Over the years I have had board members choose my successors," I explained to them, "and every time it did not turn out so well." So they agreed that I could present them with some suitable candidates. Immediately I began making lists of people I could think of. I needed someone who understood worldwide mission, and most of all had the gift of working with internationals, treating them as equals. They needed to have a good understanding of the church, but also know how to raise the funding to make an organization like *ServeNow* grow.

> I constantly heard people say, "You're so young!" or "You're too young!"

I looked among youth organizations like Youth with a Mission. I searched among internationals I knew around the world, as well as in my new homeland, the United States. After almost four months, I had not come up with one single candidate that I had 100 percent confidence in. There was a lot of prayer, as I knew that an organization would rise or fall because of the new leader.

One morning I suddenly woke up, as the Lord had clearly put a person on my heart, whom I had not even added to my list. I gently shook my wife, sleeping nicely beside me, and almost shouted, "It's Ben! It's Ben!"

She immediately responded, "No, he is too young!"

I told her, "Don't you remember what happened to us?" I had just turned 30 when our relatively calm future was drastically shaken. Out of the blue I was appointed Europe director for Living Bibles International, a worldwide organization creating modern, readable, understandable Bible translations in the major languages of the world. My areas of geographic responsibility included all of Western and Eastern Europe, as well as the Soviet Union and Israel, and I began traveling almost weekly, and often into some danger zones behind the Iron Curtain.

Two years later, just weeks before my 33rd birthday, I received a telephone call from the United States. It was the chair of the board, Victor Oliver, who cheerfully informed me that the board had appointed me the international executive director for the worldwide organization of some 139 language projects spread across every continent. We accepted the appointment the following week, with the promise I would never have to be involved in fundraising or administration and could remain in Sweden. It was still a huge challenge. Doreen was expecting our third child, Paul, within a few months. I was still involved in an intense evangelistic program for the Covenant Church of Sweden, with four-week interdenominational crusades cooperating in city after city across the country. I was also the managing director of the Swedish branch of Tyndale House Publishers.

I was simply too young for this global position and felt completely inadequate. Even remembering the names of, let alone overseeing, every one of the 139 language projects, was a daunting task. Add to that the names of the national leaders, their board members, and the translation teams working on each project.

I continued convincing my wife. "Doreen, when we said yes to that daunting task, I stepped in, being absolutely green! There was no introduction period, and no one to be a direct mentor and trainer. Ben will work with me for a few years before he steps into the presidency, and I have already seen how he handles himself in global work. Remember, I told you what happened last February when he joined me on a mission trip in India."

Usually young pastors, whom I had brought before, stood up and began their message by telling American jokes and sports stories, completely losing their audience in the first few sentences! I gave Ben an opportunity to speak to the pastors we work with, and he stood up, opened his Bible, and communicated from the Word directly to their hearts.

I was sure. I said, "He is the man, Doreen!"

Ben is chosen

Later that week, I flew out to Philadelphia and met Ben for half a day. The more we shared, the more certain I became that he was the right man. After returning home I called the chair of the board and told him that I had found a suitable candidate.

His first question was, "Lars, how old is this man?"

I answered, "He has turned 30 and will probably be 33 by the time we appoint him as president."

"Far too young!" the chair responded. Again I told him my own story and asked if I could get permission to invite Ben to the board meeting.

Permission was granted, and two months later Ben was interviewed by the board. A lively discussion followed after Ben had left the room. The age issue was brought up again, and one board member insisted we go through a search firm to find the right candidate. Another board member, who was going to step down from the board the following meeting, because of age reasons, spoke a solid word of wisdom. "Lars has heard from God regarding this young man. This young man has also heard from God. If God is not in it, it will surely fall apart very quickly. Let us accept Lars' recommendation regarding his successor."

> All leaders make mistakes, young or old. It's how they solve those mistakes that make them good, and even great leaders.

So, the vote was taken, and Ben was appointed to serve as my assistant for the foreseeable future, but no longer than to 2017. Ben assumed the presidency December 1, 2016.

Did it fall apart? No, not at all. Did Ben prove to be perfect? No, not more than any other leaders. All leaders make mistakes, young or old. It's how they solve those mistakes that make them good, and even great leaders.

11

Being a Conduit of Hope to Others

What Jesus did here in Cana of Galilee was the first of the signs through which he revealed his glory; and his disciples believed in him.
—John 2:11

We would be remiss to not devote at least one chapter challenging and encouraging you to serve now and be a vessel of hope for others in this world! If our focus is only on ourselves, then we will miss a critical means by which God provides hope in this world and replenishes our own hope in our hearts.

John 2 records Jesus' first miracle. It's the story of Jesus turning water into wine at a wedding. Here's the complete text:

On the third day a wedding took place at Cana in Galilee. Jesus' mother was there, and Jesus and his disciples had also been invited to the wedding. When the wine was gone, Jesus' mother said to him, "They have no more wine."

"Woman, why do you involve me?" Jesus replied. "My hour has not yet come."

His mother said to the servants, "Do whatever he tells you."

> *Nearby stood six stone water jars, the kind used by the Jews for ceremonial washing, each holding from twenty to thirty gallons.*
>
> *Jesus said to the servants, "Fill the jars with water"; so they filled them to the brim.*
>
> *Then he told them, "Now draw some out and take it to the master of the banquet."*
>
> *They did so, and the master of the banquet tasted the water that had been turned into wine. He did not realize where it had come from, though the servants who had drawn the water knew.* (John 2:1-9)

There is so much happening here than what first meets the eye. This first miracle turned something ordinary into something special. We can also learn from Mary's example of persistence when it comes to prayer. It's also noteworthy that she was interceding on behalf of others and not just herself. By understanding Jewish culture at that time, we can also learn that the hosts running out of wine would have been socially taboo. The result would have been intense shame for them. Jesus removes our shame! Wine is also a symbol of joy. Jesus has come to restore our joy to overflowing!

Jesus uses ordinary things

I want to focus on the method Jesus used during this miracle. Here again, he could have just made wine appear out of nothing and handled this entirely himself. But did you catch that he utilized the servants standing nearby? While they obviously were not the ones who turned the water into wine, they were the ones who played a role as this miracle unfolded. Their actions and obedience to Jesus' instructions contributed to the event. They heeded the wonderful advice of his mother, *do whatever he tells you* (v. 5). And Jesus never asked them to do something they were not capable of doing. He asked them to do two simple things: First, Jesus asked them to fill nearby empty jars with water. Then he told them to draw some out and take it to the master of the banquet. Somewhere along the lines of them acting on those two instructions, a miracle happened, and the water turned into wine. How cool is that?

Sometimes we overcomplicate things. Jesus is looking for servants who will simply do whatever he instructs them to do, no matter how much it may make sense or not! But as Lars is fond of quoting, "We cannot do what only God can do, but God will not do for us what he calls us to do."[1] In other words, as we do what God has called us to do, he will do for us what only he can do!

Jesus never asked them to do something they were not capable of doing.

When I first joined the staff of *ServeNow,* Lars told me:

> Ben, for many years I hated challenging people to give to the work I was involved in. I felt that I was begging and prayed that the Lord would just speak to people without my involvement. Then, one day, it dawned on me that my task was not to force anyone to give, and not to feel rejected if they said no. My job was to simply ask how they could use more of their resources for God's kingdom. If they said no, it was not to me, but to God who would talk to them about the answer to my question. So today, I cannot wait to ask anyone I meet about taking part in spreading God's kingdom and then wait to see what God can do.

It's one thing to be a recipient of a miracle. But it's completely different to be an instrument through which God works a miracle on behalf of others! This is the privilege of being a servant. John is careful to note that the master of the banquet, *did not realize where it had come from, though the servants who had drawn the water knew* (v. 9).

Let me ask you. What is the greater privilege and joy? Yes, it's fantastic when God works miracles in our lives. But it's even more significant when God works wonders through us in other people's lives! In many ways, Jesus said and taught that *It is more blessed to give than to receive* (Acts 20:35).

This is true because a servant gets the privilege of having a "behind the scenes" view of miracles unfolding. Sometimes, we think miracles just happen. However, there is also the reality of the miracle process, when God uses specific actions of ours that help unfold the miracle.

The results are not always immediate

Both Lars and I have spent a significant amount of time cultivating relationships with donors in many different states around the United States. There is a particular process in fundraising. Letters are drafted, materials put together, visions cast, communication efforts synchronized, stories shared, needs expressed, etc. While there is, of course, "the moment" of a gift being given, often, there was activity before that which played a role in the process. Sometimes that can be years of cultivating relationships. Just a few years ago Lars found out what happened with two gentlemen in Texas whom he had befriended for many years. Every time he visited in their city, he would meet with them either separately or together. They showed tremendous interest as Lars spoke with them, but when he challenged them about participating, they both tended to stare out in space as if they had not heard the question. After Lars moved on to *ServeNow*, he lost touch with these gentlemen until he found out they both had died. He also learned each man had left approximately a million dollars to the organization Lars was with when he knew them.

When a gift is given, it's processed, and programs are implemented. There again, those programs have often gone through a "behind the scenes" process of launching. Many details and actions are tended too. From the outside, or for those who benefit from the gift, they may see or experience the impact but have no idea the process behind it. Many of the recipients of others' generosity never even personally meet or know the donors! And most of us never know the process it took for the donor to obtain that funding to give it. We just benefit from it and know the joy of the gift!

God wants us all to serve now

The point is, God is calling us to be servants who serve now! He invites us into the process of seeing miracles unfold. He calls us to be an "empty vessel" available for him to fill and use to bring hope to others in need. And it's part of our own healing and finding our hope restored. One way God delivers us from despair and depression is by us focusing on serving others. Here is how Isaiah 58:6-9 puts it:

> *Is not this the kind of fasting I have chosen:*
> *to loose the chains of injustice*
> *and untie the cords of the yoke,*
> *to set the oppressed free*
> *and break every yoke?*
> *Is it not to share your food with the hungry*
> *and to provide the poor wanderer with shelter—*
> *when you see the naked, to clothe them,*
> *and not to turn away from your own flesh and blood?*
> *Then your light will break forth like the dawn,*
> *and your healing will quickly appear;*
> *then your righteousness will go before you,*
> *and the glory of the LORD will be your rear guard.*
> *Then you will call, and the LORD will answer;*
> *you will cry for help, and he will say: Here am I.*

If your hope is diminished, provide hope to others through your actions by meeting specific needs you see! Remember, when we stand before Jesus, we will be rewarded based on what we have done. And serving others in need is the way we serve Jesus and demonstrate our love for him. Jesus told us this in Matthew 25:31-36:

> *When the Son of Man comes in his glory, and all the angels with him, he will sit on his glorious throne. All the nations will be gathered before him, and he will separate the people one from another as a shepherd separates the sheep from the goats. He will put the sheep on his right and the goats on his left.*
>
> *Then the King will say to those on his right, "Come, you who are blessed by my Father; take your inheritance, the kingdom prepared for you since the creation of the world. For I was hungry and you gave me something to eat, I was thirsty and you gave me something to drink, I was a stranger and you invited me in, I needed clothes and you clothed me, I was sick and you looked after me, I was in prison and you came to visit me."*

Jesus takes very personally how we treat others! That is why when we serve others in need, we are really serving Jesus himself. That is a sacred privilege and responsibility! God wants to use ordinary people like you and me to become a conduit of hope for others through our actions.

> **If your hope is diminished, provide hope to others through your actions by meeting specific needs you see!**

Dreams coming true

Let me share with you a beautiful story out of Ukraine. For a couple of years, our directors there shared with me the dream of a refugee woman from the warzone in eastern Ukraine. She was forced to flee and start life all over. Thankfully, she was able to put herself through a cosmetology course. She had a dream, though, of opening her own salon. But she also wanted to teach and train other women in need, knowing there were many other women in desperate need of learning a skill. Over 1.5 million people have become internally displaced people in the dispute over the Eastern border between Russia and Ukraine. Since 2014 there have been no end of battles along the border. In the summer of 2020 the Ukrainian government forces and pro-Russian rebels began a "full and comprehensive" cease-fire following the six-year conflict that has resulted in the deaths of more than 14,000 soldiers, separatists, and civilians.

For a couple of years, that woman's dream sat on my desk in the form of a one-page paper on the idea of helping this woman train a group of women to open their own salon. Eventually, *ServeNow* was able to commit to this dream, and now it's a beautiful and fully operational salon! I have been there personally and even had my nails done for the first time!

While awkward in a way for me, it was incredibly meaningful to meet the teacher and owner myself, hear the girls' stories, and encourage a new class that was beginning their training at the time of our visit. One of the new students, for example, shared how she grew up in an orphanage, but her two daughters were at one of our summer camps a couple years before and now go to a local church!

Another student lost her husband and was pregnant at the time with their third baby, who died tragically. She is also a refugee from the war zone. It was touching to later read a post of hers on Facebook where she stated:

> These beautiful people who help me to gain a new profession!
> I am grateful to every good people who are now in my life.
> You people helped, and that helped me not to fall into depression! Your support was a lifesaver for me! Thank you for

my new life and new awesome friends! I believe that now I will be fine, and my dream will let go!

Another woman who graduated in the first class came up afterward and shared how the school has changed her life. She will be helping teach the new women as they begin their training! She even received a grant from the European Union to purchase specialized equipment to offer more services and make more money!

My point is not to say how wonderful *ServeNow* is. The real point of this story is how a refugee woman had a dream to be a "conduit of hope" for other women, despite her own depressing situation. If not for her dream and commitment, so many other women may not have found hope! Our actions and lives really can make a difference for other people.

12

The Ingredients of Hope: Anger, Compassion, Courage, and Vision

Hope has two beautiful daughters; anger and courage: anger at the way things are, and courage to struggle to create things as they should be.
—Saint Augustine of Hippo

When you look at the world today, what makes you angry?

Is it that, according to Homeland Security, human trafficking is the fastest-growing criminal enterprise in the world?[1]

Is it the fact that although abortion rates have been falling in recent years, more than 100 babies are aborted per every 1,000 pregnancies?[2]

Or what about issues of prejudice, racism, and inequality? Maybe it's the fact that more than 700 million people live on less than $2 a day worldwide, while most of the world's wealth is held by the wealthiest people and countries.[3]

Or maybe it's the reality of lack of access to clean water, medical care, or education that millions of people face? Or is it that we live in a time where we are experiencing the biggest refugee crisis in human history with more than 70 million people displaced worldwide?[4]

Maybe it bothers you that one billion people lack access to the Word of God[5] or that 40 percent of the world's population is still unreached with the Good News of Jesus Christ?[6]

If you are like us at *ServeNow*, it's all the above that makes us angry!

And maybe like me, it also makes you angry that these problems affect real human beings made in God's image and those cherished people get reduced to mere political issues, agendas, and controversies. Some are more outraged over the politics of it all than the negative impact on real human life. Our priorities are out of balance, and while we live in an age of outrage, our anger seems misplaced and misdirected.

Jim Cymbala writes in the book *Storm*,

> But nowhere in the New Testament do we see the early church discussing any of that. No, they went about doing what God told them to do, continually seeking the Lord for his blessing, regardless of what political or cultural storms raged around them. That was their secret to effectiveness: They focused on the simple instructions Christ gave them and expected his grace to help them.[7]

Ed Stetzer writes in his book *Christians in the Age of Outrage,*

> While there are countless false gods in modern Western society, I see three key idols that Christians and non-Christians alike often embrace as solutions to the age of outrage. The idols of politics, identity, and personality most often tempt us to turn away from the life-giving wellspring of God's truth and seek to save ourselves. Then, when these idols are threatened, we easily slip into outrage.[8]

Others may be angered by lesser things such as their favorite sports teams not doing well. Much of our outrage is misplaced.

We get mad about things that matter little, but we don't get mad enough about the things that matter most!

The anger of God

The fact is many things in the world are not as they should be, and that should make us angry! We need to be angry about the things that make God angry. While the anger of God has fallen out of favor in many circles and we prefer to focus on God's grace, I believe that it's precisely God's anger that makes him a God of love. If God didn't get angry about injustice, would he be good and righteous?

Likewise, if injustice and unrighteousness do not bother us enough to lead to action, how can we say we are motivated by God's love, which *does not delight in evil but rejoices with the truth* (1 Corinthians 13:6). Another

> If God did not get angry about injustice, would he be good and righteous?

straightforward verse about righteousness is found in Hebrews 1:9, which quotes the Old Testament and refers to Jesus: *You have loved righteousness and hated wickedness; therefore God, your God, has set you above your companions by anointing you with the oil of joy.*

Mark Batterson, in his book *Primal,* puts it this way,

Let me ask you a question: what will kill you if you don't do it? What makes you glad or sad or mad? What puts a holy smile on your face? What causes your spirit to sob uncontrollably? What makes you pound your fist on the table out of righteous indignation? Somewhere in the mixture of that gladness, sadness, and madness is your God-ordained passion. Or maybe I should say compassion because you feel what God feels. And once you identify it, doing something about it is not optional. You can't not do something about it.[9]

Anger can mislead us

Let me be more specific and more precise. Anger without right action does no one any good. For example, when he saw the mistreatment of his people at the hand of the Egyptians (Exodus 2:11-12), Moses becomes angry and does act, but it is the wrong action. He kills an Egyptian man in response to seeing him beating a Hebrew. Today, in America, we are seeing examples of both wrong actions on behalf of some police officers toward black people, and wrong action on behalf of rioters destroying property or verbally and physically attacking and harassing people. As Martin Luther King Jr. once powerfully put it:

> Returning hate for hate multiplies hate, adding deeper darkness to a night already devoid of stars. Darkness cannot drive out darkness; only light can do that. Hate cannot drive out hate; only love can do that.[10]

It was not until 40 years later that Moses would encounter the burning love and compassion of God that would compel him to go back to Egypt and be used by God to bring about deliverance for his people.

So, anger is necessary, but only when correctly channeled. Most action that has inspired real change has arisen from initial feelings of anger and passion. Think about William Wilberforce when it came to the slave trade. Think about Mahātmā Gandhi fighting nonviolently for independence in India. Think about civil rights leaders in the United States protesting segregation and racism. Anger over current reality compelled these leaders to fight for change in the future.

Combine your anger with action and compassion

The real challenge is combining anger with meaningful action, compassion with courage. Some people have anger but no action other than perhaps posting things all day long on social media. While there is a place for information and awareness, we live in a culture saturated with information but little meaningful action.

Others have sympathy for others but no passion to act on those sentiments. Yet, genuine compassion always results in prayer and action, perhaps best modeled in recent times by people such as Mother Teresa.

Take a look at this passage from the Gospel of Matthew:

When he saw the crowds, he had compassion on them, because they were harassed and helpless, like sheep without a shepherd. Then he said to his disciples, "The harvest is plentiful, but the workers are few. Ask the Lord of the harvest, therefore, to send out workers into his harvest field. (Matthew 9:36-38)

Likewise, when Jesus saw the crowds, he was motivated to raise the awareness level of his disciples, called them to pray, and then he empowered them to personally go (Matthew 10).

Finding solutions in the midst of problems

When we look at the world today, what do we see? Do we simply see problems or people in need? Do we see what is, but also what *could be*? In the book *Seizing Your Divine Moment*, Erwin McManus writes,

I think it's important to add that while God has been working in human history since he breathed life into Adam, there are many things yet to be done, and beyond this, many things yet to be begun. There may be another question that needs to be asked beyond, 'What is God doing?' and that is this: 'What is God dreaming?' [11]

I don't know about you, but this gets my heart pumping with a sense of holy excitement! I want to challenge you to dream the dreams of God! In the introduction of the book *Entrepreneurial Faith*, the authors make the point that "We never want to be limited by what already exists. We aspire instead to pursue what should be."[12]

Mark Batterson writes in his book *Chase the Lion*, "You have to go after a dream that is destined to fail without divine intervention."[13]

Ronnie Wilson, the pastor of our church, Gathering Stones Community Church in Falcon, Colorado, is a dreamer like this. Years ago, he and his family moved to this new community with a calling to plant a church in the area. During that time, they recognizing a need and caught a vision for starting a quality school in the community. However, this was an ambitious dream way beyond their resources, abilities, or knowledge. Many people thought they were crazy, and there were those who left the church over this vision. However, after several years of hard work, many tears, and a steep learning curve, this dream became reality! A charter school was birthed in the community that my children and many others now benefit from. In his own words, Ronnie will tell you that there were many miracles along the way that can only be explained by God's intervention:

> The beauty of God's dream is that it originates with him and he graciously reveals his dream with us! The miracles that we witnessed are to be expected because only God can fulfill his dream. When my resources were not enough, I had to fully depend on God and walk by faith rather than sight.
>
> I found myself, on several occasions, in the position of having to dismiss the dreams of others. There were many who had ideas to contribute; however, I knew I had to obey and follow God's dream and be careful not to replace it with another—including my own! All this makes God-sized dreams both exciting and terrifying. In fact, God's dreams can push us into very uncomfortable places. God-sized dreams de-

mand more than our limited experience, gifts, and abilities can accomplish alone. This reality can make a God-sized dream feel more like an uncomfortable nightmare!

I don't know about you, but I can certainly relate to the challenge and joy of God-seized dreams! I mentioned in chapter 5 that as we continued to pray and dream with our leaders at *ServeNow*, we decided to put together a three-year vision plan that could be used as a document to present before those supporting *ServeNow* or interested in partnering with us. At the time of this writing, we recently wrapped up the first year of that plan, and to our complete surprise and joy, we hit our first-year goal, which was one million dollars more than our budget was the prior year!

Dreams are becoming a reality! Hope is being realized. And reality for many people around the world is changing because people are taking action and daring to dream. One young mother in Nepal shared the following testimony with us during one of the six-month tailoring programs we host for women at risk. These programs drastically alter the future of these young women's lives and families. She said,

> My marriage fell apart, and I was left to look after my son. However, because of *ServeNow's* tailoring training program, I can now work from home and make a steady income. I am so thankful that I had the opportunity to learn a skill that has enabled me to be independent!

I love this! This single mother was facing a challenging future. However, with a vision and dream to empower those in situations like this, her future was altered.

By the way, did you know that the word "dream" in Old English originally meant "joy" or "music"?[14] In other words, a dream is a song or a melody that delights the heart. It makes your heart sing.

Make your heart sing!

We could reverse the question asked at the beginning of this chapter of "what makes you angry" to the way Steve Jobs put it, "What makes your heart sing?" If you could change something in the world, what would make you happiest? What would make God's heart sing? Carmine Gallo, in an article titled, "Steve Jobs: What Makes Your Heart Sing?" reminds us that, "There's a saying, Don't die with the music still in you."[15]

One definition that the *Merriam-Webster Dictionary* gives of the word dream is "to consider the possibility of." Not all dreams just plop down out of heaven while you are passively asleep.

What makes your heart sing?

Many dreams begin with a stirring, a churning in your heart. You begin to contemplate the possibility of something that might even defy or supersede rationality or logic. Dreams give birth to vision. Andy Stanley puts it this way in his book *Visioneering:*

> Visions are born in the soul of a man or woman who is consumed with the tension between what is and what could be. Anyone who is emotionally involved—frustrated, brokenhearted, maybe even angry—about the way things are in light of the way they believe things could be, is a candidate for a vision.[16]

Mark Batterson writes in his book *Primal,*

> Lack of faith is not a failure of logic. It's a failure of imagination. Lack of faith is the inability or unwillingness to entertain thoughts of a God who is able to do immeasurably more than all we can ask or imagine.[17]

Imagine if people didn't "dream" of things that were not yet reality at that time. There are all kinds of breakthroughs or inventions that we cannot imagine living without now such as the ability to fly in airplanes or to develop cures for various diseases.

And we all know how inspiring hearing the dreams of others can be. Martin Luther King Jr.'s "I Have a Dream" speech is one the most vivid modern examples. President John F. Kennedy's speech that is now known as "We Choose to Go to the Moon" is another example. Both painted a compelling picture of a reality that could be or what a new kind of future should look like.

I love the movie *The Greatest Showman*. One of the songs at the beginning of the film is a song called "A Million Dreams." One part of the lyrics goes like this,

> *A million dreams are keeping me awake*
> *I think of what the world could be.*

Living by the dreams in your heart

When was the last time you dreamed with that kind of childlike wonder? When was the last time you lived not by what your logical mind can make sense of but by the dream in your heart?

Dreams communicate or engage us on a whole different level. They are images that ignite the imagination. They are pictures or visions that stir the heart and propel to action. They churn relentlessly and passionately within until ready to be birthed without. They spark a sense of awe, wonder, and contemplation that something could just be possible after all that might not have prior been considered possible.

What song does God want to give you? What melody of heaven has he already placed deep inside you that he wants to be heard through your life? Can you hear God's song for your life? Is your heart tuned to his heart and to the melody, the message, and the dream he wants to give you and display through you?

Or perhaps you have lost your song. Maybe at one time there was a song in your heart that has now been lost because of pain, discouragement, disappointment, or suffering. I want to encourage you that God wants to restore that song or put a new song in your heart! He is a God of restoration, and he has a dream for our lives and in every season of our lives, no matter the disappointments or seeming limitations.

I love how Lars read the promise from Joel 2 that Peter applied to the outpouring of the Spirit in Acts 2 and took to heart the part that said, *your old men will dream dreams* (v. 17). Lars thought, "Well, I am old, and I can still dream dreams!" As a result, *ServeNow* was born! *ServeNow* is the result of a dream, a song in the heart of our founder!

Mark Batterson writes in *Primal,*

> As Christ followers we need to take a why not approach to life. It dares to dream. It's bent toward action. And it's not looking for excuses not to do something.[18]

It's dreams that produce passion and passion that sparks dreams. Passion and dreams provide focus and purpose. They display something of the person of Christ through our lives to others. He has plans to use us in unique ways that showcase the beauty of his character, demonstrate the depths of his grace, display the richness of his heart, and communicate his message of salvation, redemption, and restoration to the world.

These dreams are discovered as we seek God himself, the Great Dreamer, and a Dream Giver. There is no one more creative, joyful, beautiful, expressive, redemptive, and passionate!

As we tune our hearts to his heart, he begins to awaken us to his song. We start to move to his rhythm and beat. We start to dance to his melody. We become instruments that bring music back into others' lives. We are not to keep a distance from suffering but enter the suffering of others, as he did on our behalf. We are not to ignore the pain and brokenness of others, but with compassion in our hearts, we reach out to them with the promise of God's power to bring beauty from ashes. We are called to restore the song of salvation in all the world, for all people! We are called to set the oppressed free, break the

> These dreams are discovered as we seek God himself, the Great Dreamer, and a Dream Giver.

chains of injustice, and bring healing to the hurting and hope to the hopeless (Isaiah 58). *We are to let [our] light shine before others* (Matthew 5:16), *do good to all people* (Galatians 6:10), and *preach the gospel to all creation* (Mark 16:15).

How does the song sound in your heart?

What does this specifically look like for you? *For we are God's handiwork, created in Christ Jesus to do good works, which God prepared in advance for us to do* (Ephesians 2:10). He has saved us to serve. He has put a new song in our hearts that we might sing and speak of his grace so that others might be saved. He has extraordinary and unique ways he wants to use each of us as we seek him for his will for our lives.

In the 2017 Wonder Woman movie, Diana got it right:

> I used to want to save the world. To end war and bring peace to mankind. But then, I glimpsed the darkness that lives within their light. I learned that inside every one of them, there will always be both. The choice each must make for themselves—something no hero will ever defeat. I've touched the darkness that lives in between the light. Seen the worst of this world, and the best. Seen the terrible things men do to each other in the name of hatred, and the lengths they'll go to for love. Now I know. Only love can save this world. So I stay. I fight, and I give . . . for the world I know can be. This is my mission now. Forever.[19]

We live in such an exciting, remarkable, complicated, and unique time in human history. While the world grows darker and evil increases, there is another reality at play. The Spirit of God is at work around the world in some of the most remarkable ways! It's true that where the darkness is darkest, his light can and does shine the brightest (Isaiah 60:1-3). We can choose to focus on the darkness or focus on the opportunities and ways God's light could shine in those very places!

In a book called *Glocalization*, Bob Roberts has a chapter titled "Follow Jesus on CNN." He opens that chapter by explaining what this means,

> I believe wherever hell is breaking loose is God's way of saying to people who love him and want to follow him, 'Over Here!'

He goes on to ask this question,

> If the physical presence of Jesus were here today, where would he be? If he were ministering, serving, healing, teaching—where would he go?[20]

Why is it better to be alive now than when Jesus was here physically?

Have you ever wished you were there when Jesus walked this earth in the flesh? Yet did you know we should not wish for that, because we have it "better" than his disciples did? Think about it. When Jesus was in the flesh, he was "limited" in that sense to one place at one time, just like the rest of us. But the Spirit is not limited in that he can be everywhere at once and with everyone all the time! Jesus said to his disciples in John 16:6-7: *Rather, you are filled with grief because I have said these things. But very truly I tell you, it is for your good that I am going away. Unless I go away, the Advocate will not come to you; but if I go, I will send him to you.* Jesus was speaking of this time as a "privileged" time to live in!

God has saved you for something special

And God has not just saved us out of something but into something special. Erwin McManus has good advice when he writes in *Seizing Your Divine Moment*:

> Not every divine opportunity will create a new ministry or organization, but that really isn't the point. Every divine opportunity is born out of the power to do good. The fuel of doing good can range from passion to compassion to commitment to serve others. The Scriptures provoke us to do good toward others when it is in our power to do so. And sometimes a simple act of grace toward another human being becomes the window through which God pulls us into his future for us.[21]

Later he writes, "The key is not the ability to read God's mind, but to know his heart."[22]

So how do we know God's heart? Knowing God's heart begins when we start to delight ourselves in God and his word. Over time, his heart will then become our heart. And when we align our will with his will and his Spirit is poured out upon us as he shows us what he has in mind for us, amazing things begin to happen!

Those God is looking to use in special ways

God is not looking to use only the smartest, wealthiest, most influential, most connected, or educated people. He certainly can and does want to use those in those categories. But there are certain conditions he requires: A humility or dependency on him. A surrendered and willing heart. A person who dares to believe and begins to seek him intentionally with passion and perseverance. God says in Psalm 2:8, *Ask me, and I will make the nations your inheritance, the ends of the earth your possession.* In the book of James 4:2-3, we are informed that *you do not have because you do not ask God. When you ask, you do not receive, because you ask with wrong motives, that you may spend what you get on your pleasures.*

The Spirit of God is given to those who believe. And for those who believe, he begins to give dreams and visions of what he wants to accomplish through our lives by his Spirit. It may seem crazy to us, but nothing is too hard for him! What could it be that he wants to accomplish through your life? What God-sized dreams has he given you? What good works (God-works) does he have prepared for you to walk in?

Where do we begin?

Look around! The harvest is plentiful, but the workers are few. There are opportunities to serve everywhere. Some are big. Some are small. Some are close to us, others far away. But all matter and can make a difference in the lives of others. Ask God to reveal his plans for your life. Dare to dream. Ask him to give you his heart and His vision for your life. Ask him to fill you with his Spirit and send you out in his power, with his Spirit upon you. Ask him to do what only he can do in and through your life for the good of others and to bring glory to his great name!

> There are opportunities to serve everywhere. Some are big. Some are small. Some are close to us, others far away. But all matter and can make a difference in the lives of others.

13

Jesus Christ—the Hope of the World

A bruised reed he will not break,
and a smoldering wick he will not snuff out,
till he has brought justice through to victory.
In his name the nations will put their hope.
—Matthew 12:20-21

Do any of the worthless idols of the nations bring rain?
Do the skies themselves send down showers?
No, it is you, LORD our God.
Therefore our hope is in you,
for you are the one who does all this.
—Jeremiah 14:22

The ice cracked under my feet as I (Lars) and my hooligan friends jumped from one huge piece of ice to another. The floes covered the waterway between the large island and the mainland where I lived in Stockholm. Fearing I would be left behind I tried to jump over a major gap between the floes and missed it! Fortunately, it was not deep, but in the subzero temperature wet clothes do not feel good. What would I tell my parents? The whole gang helped me to dry land, and then we headed for the basement corridor in our apartment building where huge radiators were blasting out heat.

Earlier that day we had been scaring some old ladies by jumping up behind them and shouting the loudest we could. Many of them began to run in panic while they dropped their handbags. We didn't steal anything, but it was such fun to see their bewildered faces!

Still soaking wet, I made it to my apartment and realized it was confession time. I was close to 13 years old and already six foot three! My parents were dedicated believers, which was rather uncommon in the part of the city where we lived. The buildings were crowded with small apartments; ours was one of the larger ones, all of 660 square feet, which housed my parents, my sister (who was my elder by five years) and me.

While I had been going to Sunday school since I was three years old and attended no end of evangelistic meetings as a child, I was ashamed of my parents' faith. Being worried that any of my friends would find out we were "religious people," I made sure that any sign of such behavior was hidden in our apartment when any friends came over. Away with the hymnals and the Bibles. Any religious books I threw into the closet! I didn't want to become like my parents for anything! But deep inside, I felt ashamed, miserable, and hopeless, especially as I was a poor student and heaped in guilt.

The road to conversion

In the spring of 1957 a massive evangelistic effort took place among most of the churches in Stockholm. From January until the first week of March, meetings based on the Billy Graham model of crusades were held in a massive church, which had two sets of balconies. These services happened every night except Mondays and Tuesdays. An extended choir space was built as the choir had hundreds of members; the choir was accompanied by a small orchestra. My sister and my parents sang in the choir, and every night before the evangelistic service began, they practiced for an hour, and I simply had to come along. I sat in the

> Deep inside, I felt ashamed, miserable, and hopeless, especially as I was a poor student, and heaped in guilt.

most remote corner of the second balcony, trying to do my homework while they practiced.

Somehow I had a love-hate relationship to this crusade. I was fascinated by the dramatic preaching, the atmosphere as people walked forward to commit their lives to Christ, and by the lively, inspiring music. But I also hated the public awareness this crusade was creating in my neighborhood. It made headline news in the secular press and most of the time the coverage was not very positive. People in general were talking about it, friends at school asked about it and the boys on the street knew that somehow the "religious Dunbergs" had to be associated with it in one form or another.

I fought against the message preached every night. It was personal and radical, and it cut into the bare bones of my being. As we traveled home by streetcar every night, my parents would hint to me: "Lars, don't you think that this is the right time for you to commit your life to Christ?" My mother's eyes would well up with tears and her voice trembled a bit, and I felt extremely awkward. The more they hinted, the more uncomfortable I became. I simply wanted to be left alone and sort out my faith or the lack thereof on my own.

I was determined not to listen to any of the sermons that were presented by a team of very gifted evangelists, and I tried to block them out night after night. As people were invited to come forward to be counseled, I sneered at their foolishness while I sank deeper down in my own personal misery!

Finally, the next-to-last night of the crusade came. It was the second day of March 1957. I had now moved from the back corner in the top balcony to the front row, being able to peer down on the crowds on the main floor. Rev. Berthil Paulsson, Sweden's Billy Graham, was preaching that night, and suddenly I felt that his message was only for me. "He who comes to me I will certainly not throw out," echoed the words through the massive church. That was not the reverend speaking to me, that was Jesus! As I heard Jesus speaking to me, I suddenly realized I was the biggest sinner in the world. Was it true that Jesus would receive even me? When the invitation to receive Christ was given directly after the message I could hardly wait to rush down to the front of the church where the preacher would lead the people coming forward in the sinner's prayer and then let counselors take over. They would take the group to a private room, lead you through a prayer, and then provide some basic helps, as well as explain about a correspondence Bible study you could work through.

Unfortunately, in my eagerness to get down from the balcony, I took the wrong staircase, opened the door in front of me, which I believed led to the main sanctuary of the church, but found myself out on the street! At that point it would have been easier to just go home, but I turned around, hurried through the appropriate door and walked forward with many others. As Rev. Paulsson prayed the prayer for us to commit our lives to Jesus, I prayed with all the sincerity of a teenager's heart. In the counseling room I struggled through the first sheet of the correspondence Bible course, designed by the Navigators. It was not very user friendly for my age group, and I felt very embarrassed that I didn't quite understand all the questions. But I knew without a doubt that my life had been transformed, not by the preacher's words or the counselor's prayer, but by Jesus Christ. My Savior had lifted me out of a literal pit of despair and hopelessness and provided a brand new life within, which gave me hope for the future.

Calling becomes a reality

It was clear to me that I could hardly wait to share my faith. I simply had to become an evangelist. Although difficult at first, I began sharing my faith at school with my friends and found to my surprise that quite a few of the people in my class at school also had parents who went to church, and that they went with them.

> I knew without a doubt that my life had been transformed, by Jesus Christ, who had lifted me out of a literal pit of despair and hopelessness and provided a brand new life within, which gave me hope for the future.

Somehow, they had never let anyone know that they were in the same boat as I was.

About a year after my conversion, the church that my parents belonged to decided it was time to renovate some of their facilities. One of their decisions was to close a little library, which had been maintained for many years. Seeing a pile of hundreds of books lying outside of what had been the library, I went to the pastor and asked if I could buy these books. We set a price of $15 and more than 300 titles changed hands. Many of them were very old, but among them were several books that in time would shape my entire life.

As I carried the books home over a couple of days, I began to realize what I had purchased. There were biographies of Dwight L. Moody and Ira Sankey, William Carey, Charles Spurgeon, Billy Sunday, and Hudson Taylor. There were books describing the revivals sweeping across Europe in the 19th century, Swedish revival history, and the stories of Charles Finney and Jonathan Edwards.

I was especially fascinated by Dwight L. Moody, Charles Spurgeon, and Billy Sunday. Moody had filled the largest auditoriums across the United States and Britain, yet he was an unlearned man. I could identify with him. Among the collection was a book of Ira Sankey's hymns, and I sang them to myself in my room. I also studied the pictures in the books and now and then practiced the preacher's gestures in front of the mirror. Who would become a Dwight Moody or a Billy Sunday or even a Billy Graham in my generation?

Charles Spurgeon was special too because he never went to seminary but he loved to read, just like me. Often he had to use other buildings than his church, as so many people flocked to hear him. London's Crystal Palace Exhibition was a massive glass structure seating 30,000 people, and his voice was so loud that it could carry across the entire audience. He had a sermon for every situation.

And then there was Billy Sunday. I carefully copied many of his sayings down in a book and memorized them. Here was a man who called sin "sin," who could speak with his whole body, catch the crowds, and hold them. I read, prayed, and cried, "Lord, raise up new people like Moody, Spurgeon, Sunday, and Graham!" As I read through these old, dusty books with these stories of conversions, church growth, victories, and setbacks, I was awed by the original personalities who dared to stand up, take risks, and be counted whatever the cost. I was deeply moved. It was as if God was speaking to me through the pages and the characters: "Lars, I will do it again, I will do it again."

When I was 10 years old, my grandmother, who was in her 90s at that time, prayed a prayer holding my hand, from her sickbed. It was a prayer I did not understand then. She prayed, "Lars, you will preach to thousands." As I read these books, her prayer kept ringing in my ears! I can clearly say that apart from the Word of God nothing impacted me more in my youth than God's Work through people's lives in the rich history of the church.

During these formative years, my parents brought me along to many different kinds of services in various denominational churches. Churches in Sweden in those days seemed to cooperate much more, and so many churches exhibited such a drive to share the gospel. As our own church never had services on Saturdays, and Sunday night services became scarce, we often would visit the huge Philadelphia Church, which had 7,000 members, to hear visiting preachers from England or the United States. I was always fascinated by how the interpreters could be so quick to translate the meaning of what just had been said. I never dreamed that I would preach there myself in the future.

I will do it again, I will do it again.

At an early age I realized that while we may have some theological idiosyncrasies and see some issues from different angles, we Christians are really a large family that will live together in eternity. This understanding was an immense help as I became active in inter-denominational activities through most of my ministry years.

At every opportunity where there was a crusade, I would go night after night, listen and be moved to tears as the invitation to come forward was given. During the summers, such crusade meetings were held in huge circus-like tents with sawdust on the floor. Kerosene heaters or generators pumped in heated air. There is no smell like the smell of a Swedish tent crusade! Later in life I would conduct many crusade meetings in that kind of atmosphere.

Joining an army

Through a neighbor I was invited to visit The Salvation Army, which actually is a very evangelical church. This organization learned early that the Bible needs to be in one hand and the glass of cold water in the other! I had read some books about their pioneers who were fiery evangelists. As I studied the pages of Army history, many stories came to the forefront and impregnated into me the fact that risk-taking, boldness, holiness, and being somewhat a fool for Christ would bring others into the Kingdom. The question that grew within me was simply, "How do I enroll in such an Army?" When I turned 15, I became a member of the local Salvation Army church, and my eagerness to serve God kept increasing.

During this time in High School, the Lord began to speak to me clearly, and I listened as only a teenager can. I knew that the Lord wanted me to serve him full-time, but at that time I was only 16 years old. They didn't have 16-year old preachers even in The Salvation Army! To enter their training college for full-time service I needed to be at least 18 years old. Over and over the words from Luke 9:23-25 came to me:

> *Then he said to them all: "Whoever wants to be my disciple must deny themselves and take up their cross daily and follow me. For whoever wants to save their life will lose it, but whoever loses their life for me will save it. What good is it for someone to gain the whole world, and yet lose or forfeit their very self?"*

I knew I had heard Jesus say, "Follow me" in my life and I knew he was calling me. But how could that happen? Long discussions followed with my parents. From a theological and practical standpoint I worked hard at convincing them that algebra and English had nothing to do with following Jesus, were not needed for me to become a preacher, and would certainly not bring anyone into the Kingdom of God!

The message of Luke 9 became so crystal clear that as I left for school every morning, I used to leave all the Bibles I could find at home opened to Luke 9:62, so my mother could come to the same understanding that *No one who puts his hand to the plow and looks back is fit for service in the kingdom of God.* The words were etched into my teenage heart. The world was literally without hope, and I was stuck in school with the solution! The emotions within me were so strong that I couldn't sleep at night; I daydreamed at school—and kept on struggling with English, German, French, and math! All my final exams that year in those four subjects came back, marked "failed," and more than one parent-teacher conference was held on my behalf.

Finally my mother knew that there had to be a solution to release this tension within me. She and I went for a long walk and talked it through. While I was in my second year toward the foundational Swedish exam to enter university, there was at that time another lower type exam available, which you could take at 17. After some discussion with the school principal, I was allowed to step down into this lower form of schooling and suddenly found myself with only four months of schooling left. It became a golden opportunity for fast education! Suddenly my English improved and so did my German. I had already studied the level of math required, and therefore, I could graduate with honors in the spring of 1961.

After applying for a job with the Swedish Internal Revenue service, I was hired as a tax assistant to work in the department dealing with delinquent alimony payments from divorced fathers. In those days, these payments were collected right out of the fathers' paychecks even before the income tax was paid. At 17 I was placed in charge of a small department with four ladies working with me and learned from scratch what it means to manage something. My goal was to earn enough money to be able to attend The Salvation Army College for Officer Training.

Beginning preaching

During this time I had my first preaching opportunity, which almost turned out to be my last. One Monday morning, a pastor in The Salvation Army called to inform me that she would be gone the following Sunday. "Lars, can you come and take the service?" The small town was not more than 25 miles away from Stockholm, and I immediately said yes, sensing that this was an invitation from God to "try my wings."

That whole week I hardly ate anything, not because of a deeply rooted spirituality leading me to a week-long fast, but because of nervousness. I borrowed my father's Bible because it was rather big and looked impressive. I found a book of sermons by an old Army veteran and carefully chose the one that I felt was the hottest subject: "Flee for your life" was the Lord's message to Lot in Genesis 19, as he attempted his escape from the condemned city of Sodom.

Although I had memorized the entire sermon, I felt the delivery was a disaster. If this was what it was like to preach, I would never again stand up in front of a crowd. I returned home feeling utterly spent and a complete failure. A few days later the phone rang again. It was another Salvation Army pastor and he called to tell me that he had heard that I had spoken in church the Sunday before. "Can you come and speak and bring a group of musicians with you for a long weekend?" And so it started. Sunday after Sunday I would be out in different places, sharing Christ, and learning to put messages together. I was eager to share the burden God had given me from the Word.

After working for a year, I had scraped together enough money to pay for the tuition at The Salvation Army College for Officer Training as well as having all the clothes and pocket money needed to leave home.

God confirms my calling

As I prepared myself for being trained for ministry, I was still struggling for assurance regarding my calling. As the time came closer to attend the college, I prayed: "God, please show me clearly that this is your will. Let me know beyond a shadow of a doubt that you want me to serve you in full-time ministry." Soon after that prayer, I was asked to conduct a Saturday night meeting at my church, where the young people would share in song and music and I would lead the service and preach. Saturday nights were not nights when many people would leave their TVs to go to church, but I wanted to take on the challenge. As the young people gathered for several weeks beforehand in prayer, I remember telling them: "We are going to hold this meeting for the Lord Jesus Christ." Handbills and posters were made, pasted on walls and circulated. As we continued to pray, our prayer was, "Lord, perform a miracle among us."

I also made a personal pledge, almost like a fleece, with the Lord. "I want to see this hall filled, and as I ask for people to come forward to seek God, let the kneeling prayer bench at the front be surrounded by people seeking your face. By this I will know that you have called me." This prayer was not prayed out of a desire to become great or famous but because I desperately needed the confirmation that the Lord could use a young and fairly uneducated person.

To my amazement the hall was filled when we walked in from the prayer meeting before the service. We shared our testimonies and songs with gusto. My sermon was taken from Acts 3:11-21, which was Peter's sermon to the onlookers in Solomon's Colonnade in the Jerusalem temple. As I invited people to come forward to dedicate their lives to the Lord at the end of my message, people lunged forward with great speed, rows after rows after rows of pews filled with people kneeling down, seeking the Lord with tears, and many gave their lives to Christ that night. With amazement I watched the Lord answer my prayer; he had strongly confirmed his purposes for my life.

My hopelessness transformed into absolute hope for the future. I have spent almost 60 years in evangelistic ministry, interwoven with organizational leadership for a variety of ministries. God has broadened my ministry platform to serve through serveral denominations in three countries. My adult life has been involved in the Word of God, evangelism, and discipleship; it has been built on the foundation that Jesus Christ was and is my only hope.

Ben's story

My parents made it a priority for our family to go to church. We faithfully attended Sunday services and Sunday school, and I was involved in youth groups and various summer camps.

Around middle school, my heart began awakening to God. At 12 years old, I found myself alone one day at my grandparents when I suddenly became aware of God's presence. At that moment, I fell to my knees, and out of my mouth came the words, "Jesus, I need you, and I want to give my life to serve you."

Immediately, I experienced an internal peace, joy, love, and hunger for God that has not dissipated. I didn't realize until years later that this was the moment I experienced what Jesus called being "born again." As Jesus explained to a religious teacher named Nicodemus in John 3:3-7, Jesus replied,

> *Very truly I tell you, no one can see the kingdom of God unless they are born again.*
> *"How can someone be born when they are old?" Nicodemus asked. "Surely they cannot enter a second time into their mother's womb to be born!"*

Jesus answered, "Very truly I tell you, no one can enter the kingdom of God unless they are born of water and the Spirit. Flesh gives birth to flesh, but the Spirit gives birth to Spirit. You should not be surprised at my saying, 'You must be born again.'"

For many reading this, you understand that Jesus is referring to the fact that just as we are physically born into this world, we must experience a spiritual birth by trusting in Jesus. That day at my grandparent's house was my spiritual birthday. While everyone's experience differs, the question is essential: have you been born again by trusting in Jesus? Jesus was clear that we must be born again, and the way to be born again is through faith in him. Jesus' answer to Nicodemus has become a well-known

> At that moment, I fell to my knees, and out of my mouth came the words, "Jesus, I need you, and I want to give my life to serve you."

verse to this day: *For God so loved the world that he gave his one and only Son, that whoever believes in him shall not perish but have eternal life. For God did not send his Son into the world to condemn the world, but to save the world through him* (John 3:16-17).

If you grew up in the church environment as I did, we were asked quite often whether we had been born again. Constant altar calls and evangelistic messages urged people to be saved and put their hope in Christ. Sadly, this doesn't seem to happen as much anymore in the United States. However, it's still the most critical question and eternity-altering experience in anyone's life.

However, this is also not where my story ends! After all, being born again is just the beginning of a new life in Christ! And just because we have been born again and have the promise of the sure hope of eternal life, we still face many trials, hardships, and struggles throughout the rest of our lives on earth.

Teen struggles

Even though my eternity was settled that day in middle school, I began to struggle with being a Christian in high school. I have always been very insecure and shy. I was embarrassed about being a Christian and had all kinds of misconceptions about what that meant and even what Jesus was really like. For years, I imagined him as a kind of weak and wimpy figure that only nerdy and wimpy people needed. I wanted to be popular, cool, and athletic!

During 11th grade, I became more and more depressed and angry, especially when my then-girlfriend Lauren (she's now my wife!) broke up with me. I remember I was so angry and depressed that one of my teachers wrote to my parents expressing concern.

It was around this time that I had a sleepover at my house with some friends. The ringleader, the most unlikely to say something like this, recommended we go to his church in the morning. By that time, I was not going to Sunday school much anymore and did not care for church. However, because this friend suggested this, I visited a different church that morning with no intention of listening.

That morning the pastor shared three baseball illustrations in his sermon. Since I loved baseball, I found myself listening! This pastor also had a passion for Jesus and was not ashamed of it. That also caught my attention, so I kept going back to this church. One Sunday, I even found myself up at the front of the altar when prayer was offered. When the pastor came to me and asked what I would like prayer for, I had no idea, but I knew I was missing something in my life!

Not long after all this, I was invited to go on a work mission trip to Tennessee with some new friends who were also athletes like me. On that trip, one of the players on my team—a guy named David Neff—and I found ourselves going for a walk one evening. We had both professed to be Christians, but we were not following Jesus. David and I acknowledged we needed to see some changes in our lives and rededicate our lives to seeking Jesus.

One dream exchanged for another

My dream up to this point in my life was also to become a major-league baseball player. Anyone who knew me at that time would note my obsession with baseball. I would be up early before school, and also out later than anybody else working out or practicing. I demanded perfection of myself and was never satisfied. And while I was good, it did not dawn on me until after my senior year that I was not good enough to make it to the major leagues. When our team lost the championship game that summer, partly due to errors I made early in the game, I entered into a period of utter despair. Somehow, I knew at that moment that it was over. And yet I had no idea what else I would do with my life. I vividly remember how hopeless and meaningless life felt. I realized that even if I did go on to play major-league baseball, at some point, it would end and then what? If baseball were my life, what would life be all about when it ended, whether now or later? I felt utterly hopeless and lost!

That Sunday at church, the pastor preached a message on the Great Commandment. In Matthew 22:37, Jesus said the greatest commandment was to *love the Lord your God with all your heart and with all your soul and with all your mind.* That morning I realized that was the true meaning of life! The next week happened to be a special week at a camp where an evangelist spoke every night. During one of those evenings, I surrendered baseball and submitted my life to whatever future God had for me. My passion shifted from baseball to God's presence, and I suddenly rediscovered real hope and meaning again.

Three things

I went off to college, still not knowing what God had for my life. But during that time, all I wanted to do was worship, be in his Word, pray, and attend Bible studies! During one of those nights alone with God, I sensed God leading me to do three things: go back home, go to Bible college, and start a Bible study with youth my age. I was excited about the first two things, but I began arguing with God over leading a Bible study. I remember saying that I was too young, didn't know enough, and was way too shy to speak in front of a group of people. But then, I read the story of Moses in Exodus 3 and realized how similar my excuses were to the ones he tried to use!

A couple of months later, I went home, started going to Lancaster Bible College, and launched a Bible study with youth my age. I did so with the help of David Neff. He became my first real "brother in Christ" as we regularly checked in on each other. He was also far more outgoing than I was, so I felt more confident when he was around.

That first week of Bible College was mission week. The theme that year was "Living in Light of Eternity." I remember being so enamored with the reality of eternity. Little did I know that it was also God's way of preparing me for the first real tragedy I would experience.

Three months after starting that Bible study and going to Bible college, I received a call one late afternoon at 5:29 p.m. It was my pastor's wife, and her voice was trembling. She went on to tell me that my friend, Dave Neff, had just been killed in a motorcycle accident.

The next week was all a whirlwind, and yet so much of it, down to little details, remain vivid memories. I was asked to speak at his funeral, where I shared his testimony. His story touched many hearts and impacted many lives. As I told you in chapter 5, our Bible study grew significantly with other youth our age attending. It was through that tragedy that Lauren began attending the study. We ended up getting back together and eventually married!

Doors also began opening for me to speak in various places and churches. I even started going on mission trips with a mission organization called Sport X Change. They travel throughout Latin American countries using sports as a way to share the Gospel. I would go on their fast-pitch softball trips, and in between games, one of us would share our testimony, and someone would share the Gospel with the other teams and fans. It was a great way to use a former passion and talent for a redemptive purpose in the lives of others rather than a selfish ambition in my life.

This entire season launched me into ministry and made me decide on pastoral ministry as my focus in college. That in turn led to pastoring a church for six years in New Jersey, which in turn led to my current role with *ServeNow*.

Not only blessings but also challenges

Through those years, I experienced the challenges we all face as we grow older and experience more of life and numerous hardships. And through various seasons, situations, struggles, failures, and disappointments, I have had to battle varying degrees of depression, discouragement, anger, and even despair or lack of hope, despite knowing and following Jesus.

I share this because merely coming to know Jesus and the eternal hope he gives doesn't mean life becomes easy. It doesn't mean we get to sidestep having ups and downs and seasons of doubts. It doesn't mean that we have the same level of hope in all seasons. Perhaps my favorite book in the Bible is Ecclesiastes. One day I hope to write a book on hope from that book! Ecclesiastes was written by a man in a season of great despair who questioned the meaning of life. I have often turned to that book because of my own battles with despair. Life can be frustrating, and there are many questions we all wrestle with. And not all questions in life are answered in the here and now.

But here is what I do know. I shudder to think of where I would be—or not be—if it weren't for the hope that is found only in Jesus Christ. Only he can offer the kind of eternal and real and lasting hope that is uniquely found in him. Everything else is temporary, fleeting, and momentary. Only he provides joy and peace that is beyond external circumstances.

My story is one of hope. Hope is what rescued me. Hope is what has saved me. Hope is what we all need. And that hope is found in Jesus Christ.

In Isaiah 49:23, we read this promise from God himself, *Then you will know that I am the LORD; those who hope in me will not be disappointed.* If you have never placed your hope entirely in Jesus, I invite you to do so. And for those of you who have placed your hope in him at some point in your life, I want to encourage you to continue placing your hope in him.

Finding hope in God requires placing our hope in God and continuing to do so. The life Jesus has for us is not about a one-time decision or even a salvation experience. That is just the start of a life of hope! He intends for us to keep putting our hope in him. And the promise here is that though we will experience various disappointments

> My story is one of hope. Hope is what rescued me. Hope is what has saved me. Hope is what we all need. And that hope is found in Jesus Christ.

in life, we will not ultimately be disappointed. All else in life will fail us. Only Jesus is forever faithful! He is the hope of the world.

When Christ has become your hope he wants to use you

The term "Great Commission" is not found in Scripture word for word. It's what historically the bidding of God "to make disciples of all nations" has been called. The reason for the name is that it sums up Jesus' final instructions to his disciples before he ascends to heaven. It's our "charge" or "commission" as his people, the mission and responsibility of all followers of Jesus. While not all of us may individually, personally, or physically "go" to another country, we are all to be involved in mission. Going, giving, and praying involves us all.

Years ago I read a statement by William Carey, one of the pioneer missionaries to India: "Attempt great things for God, expect great things from God." When he wanted to go and be a missionary, the deacons in his church told him that when God wanted to send missionaries, he could well do it without Carey. But he did go, translating the Bible into numerous Indian languages, and others have followed in his footsteps.

In the 20th century, the pastor of The Peoples Church in Toronto, Oswald J. Smith, used to say, "We talk of the Second Coming; half the world has never heard of the first."

There have been major changes in evangelical Christianity in the past 50 years. When churchgoers answer this question: Have you heard of the Great Commission? People answer as follows according to researcher George Barna:

- 51 percent say *No*
- 7 percent say *I'm not sure*
- 25 percent say *Yes, but I can't recall the meaning*

That's 83 percent of the churchgoers!

- 17 percent say *Yes, and I know what it means*[1]

The mandate for all of us is to go and make disciples, to baptize them, and to teach all nations. We can't make disciples until we share the Gospel with people. We can't baptize people unless we bring them into a saving knowledge of Christ. And we can't teach people to be followers of Jesus if they don't first commit themselves to follow him. It all begins with going! We are to go into all the world and preach the Gospel. The message we proclaim is not our own, nor is it from a particular denomination or church. It's Jesus that we preach. But we mustn't stop there. We are to teach Scripture and make disciples of people who commit themselves to Jesus and follow him. We not only call people to trust in Christ but also to devote themselves to becoming like him.

Many people view God's call to mission as a separate and often specific call that we receive years after our salvation. Perhaps you expect God's Spirit to wake you up in the middle of the night and blow you out of bed. When your nose lands on a specific location on the world map you placed on the floor next to your bed the night before, you will believe it's the location where the Lord wants you to go.

No, it isn't that simple, neither is it that complex. God wants us anywhere and everywhere! It's inherent in our call to salvation. We are all given one or more spiritual gifts and a part to play in fulfilling the Great Commission. Jesus calls us even today! *Come, follow me, . . . and I will send you out to fish for people* (Matthew 4:19). Far too many of us sit around waiting for a "voice" to tell us what God has already spelled out in a verse.

The important thing is not what we do in the mission to the world, but who we are. Jesus is the light of the world, but he has also asked us to shine. Wherever light is shining, darkness is conquered. This world operates within the kingdom of darkness. Therefore, we need to shine throughout the world with the light of God's kingdom. Jesus spoke to the people once more and said, *I am the light of the world. If you follow me, you won't have to walk in darkness, because you will have the light that leads to life* (John 8:12, NLT).

Jim Cymbala writes in the book *Storm*:

> Our problem is not with a godless, secular America, but with a church that is increasingly prayerless, compromised, demoralized, and weak. We have drifted away from the Word of God and the power of the Holy Spirit.
>
> Where will we find the grace to change? To turn things around?
>
> When will we be desperate enough to come to God just as we are, pleading for his help and ready to follow wherever he leads?
>
> In many places now, it seems we would rather blame the culture, the school system, the government, and the media rather than examine our own spiritual condition.[2]

You are created for a specific role

It's time for "ordinary believers" in our churches to discover the understanding that they are called to mission and that they are shaped by God for a specific role in that mission. The word "go" in the Great Commission means the same in every language: take one step in front of the other and present our lives for his service in obeying the Great Commission. It's only a matter of where and how. Isaiah 52:15 (NLT) says, *And he will startle many nations. Kings will stand speechless in his presence. For they will see what they had not been told; they will understand what they had not heard about.* Acts 9:15 (NLT): *The Lord said, "Go, for Saul is my chosen instrument to take my message to the Gentiles and to kings, as well as to the people of Israel."* We can all be a part of influencing the end result: people of all nations, tribes, and tongues praising God before his throne.

It's time to let Jesus open our eyes.

> *Then he opened their minds to understand the Scriptures. And he said, "Yes, it was written long ago that the Messiah would suffer and die and rise from the dead on the third day. It was also written that this message would be proclaimed in the authority of his name to all the nations, beginning in Jerusalem: 'There is forgiveness of sins for all who repent.'"* (Luke 24:45-47, NLT)

Will your eyes be open to what God plans for your life? In one of his letters to the Corinthians, the apostle Paul tells how he gave up all the rights and privileges he had in order to be more effective sharing the Gospel. The privilege to share the Gospel was so great that he would rather die than have it taken away from him.

Mission history is filled with people who gave up all their privileges to spread the Gospel. If the day ever comes when my heart does not stir for the mission to the world, the Lord needs to take me home. If you would rather do what you are good at and have studied for, sometimes at a high expense, I encourage you to continue to do so. But if the Lord has placed a fire in your heart to see people come to Christ and become disciples, then you must go, taking with you the specialty you have learned, to wherever he sends you. There is no greater task in the world than to guide people to the only hope they will ever have in this world, namely Jesus Christ.

> Joy still comes in the morning
> Hope still walks with the hurting
>
> —Matt Maher, "Alive and Breathing"[1]

Epilogue

If something has struck a chord in your heart while reading this book or if the stories have inspired you to want to engage further with *ServeNow*, allow me to provide a few meaningful next steps.

Generosity of heart and life

The term *generosity* can mean something more than giving money. Let me tell you about one of *ServeNow's* partners who has made many of the stories you read about in this book a reality. Her name is Nancy, and she's one of the most compassionate and generous people I know. When I'm with her, I always tell her, "We need a thousand more Nancys!" This is not simply because she gives generously of her finances. It's because her heart is genuinely moved by the needs of people around the world. Nancy has never traveled with *ServeNow* on a trip (yet!) and met the people her generosity has enriched. Yet, she genuinely cares and gives from her heart. This is what I mean by "a thousand more Nancys." Jesus is not after our money. He is after our hearts. And Jesus said, *But store up for yourselves treasures in heaven, where moths and vermin do not destroy, and where thieves do not break in and steal. For where your treasure is, there your heart will be also* (Matthew 6:20-21). Where are you investing your resources? Are you storing up earthly treasure that is temporary or treasure in heaven that is eternal?

Remember, it's not about what you don't have or can't do. It's about what you do have and what you can do. Recently, another one of our supporters, a widow named Barbara, called to let me know she was having surgery, and because of limited resources, she could not give financially at that time. However, she had some reward points on her credit card that she could use to obtain a gift card for us at a couple of different stores. It just so happened that we were looking to purchase something at one of the stores for an office need! I was really touched by her creative generosity. She easily could have focused on what she couldn't give or didn't have. But instead, she found a meaningful way to give what she did have and do what she could do!

Do you remember the classic story *How the Grinch Stole Christmas?* The story begins with noting how the Grinch's heart was "two sizes too small." According to an article, Christians in the United States are only giving 2.5 percent of their income.[1] Did you know this is less than what Christians in the United States gave during the Great Depression, which was 3.3 percent? But remember what happened when the Grinch had a change of heart and began showing generosity? Dr. Seuss noted that "the Grinch's small heart grew three sizes that day." Giving is not only for those who benefit from it. Giving is for the good of our own hearts. Jesus is inviting us into a life of generosity, a life where through our giving, we reflect his very nature and character. The evidence of God's love for us begins with the fact that, *For God so loved the world he gave . . .* (John 3:16). And when God gives, he does not hold back, do it half-heartedly, or give stingily. Rather, he gives all. He gives his best. He gives himself. I encourage you to be one of the thousand other Nancys who I am praying for or creative givers like Barbara! Through your generosity, you can serve people in need, show God's love to the most vulnerable, become the answer to the prayers of others, make the dreams of others a reality, and bring hope to many around the world.

Participate in a ServeNow *Mission Trip*

The second way you can become meaningfully involved in *ServeNow* is going on a mission trip with us to see the needs of the world firsthand and to meet some of the most passionate, dedicated, and inspiring leaders I know. In this book, I shared about Tanya in Ukraine, Supratim in India, Moses in Uganda, and others. They all have some of the most incredible stories of hope you will ever hear. Our director in Nepal, Arjun, for example, was orphaned at a young age. His mother died shortly after giving birth to his younger sister. His father abandoned Arjun and his two sisters, and so for a time, before being taken into an children's home, Arjun had to take care of his sisters. Arjun is a very spiritually sensitive soul. To find peace for his broken heart and loss of his mother's love, he worshiped many idols. But at the children's home, he heard about God's love for him in Jesus, and for the first time, he discovered true hope and peace in his heart.

Fast-forward years later. Today, Arjun and his wife have two children, but they've taken into their family another 18 orphans! His older sister is chairwoman of our board in Nepal and his younger sister is a staff member. Through *ServeNow* in Nepal, Arjun, his sisters, and other team members all came from seemingly hopeless situations but now serve thousands of people who also live in vulnerable situations. Together, they are introducing hundreds of children and women to the love of God in Christ. Arjun is just one example of many wonderful national leaders whom you can meet and serve alongside on a mission trip with *ServeNow*. You can use your gifts, and even just your presence, to show God's love in action to the most vulnerable. I promise you will be inspired and encouraged by what God is doing around the world!

Let me share the words of Daniel and Sandy who went on a mission trip with *ServeNow*. Daniel even became a *ServeNow* board member on this trip as well, and Sandy also has helped in volunteer capacities over the years:

> Having grown up in the church and been around mission agencies for many years, my wife and I had certainly heard of many mission trips but never thought that this would be

something we would ever do. After all, how effective could a software developer and an accountant be in a remote Asian country? All these thoughts have changed after we were able to spend 10 days in Nepal with *ServeNow*. We joined a diverse team of individuals who were able to see first-hand both the tremendous spiritual and physical needs in this country, as well as the amazing work being accomplished by the local staff. It's one thing to hear of the different program offerings like the Lighthouse Centers and the Tailoring Program but seeing the results and the impact with our own eyes made us really value this work. When you are listening to a young woman tell you the difference in her life after graduating from the Tailoring Program, and you can sense her new-found self-confidence, you truly comprehend the impact of these programs.

And the surprising thing is that the Nepali people were so glad that we visited. Wherever we traveled in the country, we were treated as "honored guests." We realized that it was not because we had some special skill or imparted some profound wisdom. They were simply thankful that someone from the U.S. cared enough to come visit them, provide blankets, and winter coverings, and offer words of hope and encouragement. In short, this trip dramatically altered our outlook on missions and allowed us to be a blessing to others. We learned that a big part of mission trips is simply showing up and sharing God's love.

Become a ServeNow *Prayer Warrior*

We are well aware that our help comes from the Lord and that apart from him we can do nothing. Over and over we have experienced miracle after miracle that can only be attributed to one thing: the prayers of God's people. One year, we had a shipment of 4,500 Christmas gifts sent through a partner ministry out of

Scotland to Ukraine. However, that year, they were held up in customs longer than expected. A team from the United States was going to give out these gifts, as this was the whole focus and purpose of the trip. Additionally, promises had been made to have these gifts to the children and others in time for the Ukrainian Christmas, which is celebrated on January 7th, according to the Orthodox calendar. With each passing day, it looked bleaker and bleaker that these gifts would get through customs on time. Finally, it became clear it would take a literal miracle for the gifts to clear customs. But a group of *ServeNow* prayer warriors began increasing their prayers for this situation and were asking God for a miracle—and God responded! Through a couple of meetings with the right custom agents that lined up in a way that even the agents noted never happens, the gifts cleared at the very last possible moment! I could tell you story after story like this that can only be attributed to God's people praying for *ServeNow*. We need an army of prayer warriors!

Become a ServeNow *Advocate*

You can give. You can go. You can pray. These are wonderful ways to meaningfully make a difference! But you can also become someone who influences, inspires, and multiplies God's work through engaging others on behalf of *ServeNow*! And don't think you have to be supergifted! All you need is a willing heart and to put a little time and thought into engaging others in your relational networks.

Steve and Kristen Manz, to whom this book is dedicated, are two such people who come to mind when I think of *ServeNow* advocates. Kristen serves on our board, and prior to that, she hosted many meetings in her home where Lars and I have shared with the Manz's friends and Bible study group. I will never forget one meeting where both Lars and I shared stories from around the world and about some projects we were involved in. Toward the end, one gentleman spoke up and directly asked us how much blankets cost to get to those in need. I nervously shared the amount. To our great surprise and joy, he immediately said, "I will give a gift for 1,000 blankets!" Then, he asked how much sewing machines for graduates of our tailoring classes cost and how many girls were graduating in an upcoming class. Again, I hesitantly shared the need as he responded, "And we will provide the sewing machines for that entire class!" His generosity influenced others to give as well, but none of this would have happened if Steve and Kristen hadn't opened their home to allow us to come share with a group of their friends.

The wild part about that night was when I informed our director in India about the gift for blankets, he told me the most amazing testimony. He was in a very remote region and that very day had come across a village where they were praying for blankets! As we had already fulfilled what we had funding to complete that year, we both thought we were finished until next year. But that night, God heard the prayers of some people in need in a remote village of India and answered it through a couple at a home meeting in Texas, who graciously opened their home to us and their friends to hear more about *ServeNow*.

We never know how God might use us, but he can only use those who are willing!

I encourage you to contact us at info@weservenow.org or 719-900-1800 to discuss ways you can become a *ServeNow* advocate. Check out our website as well at www.weservenow.org to find out more or to order some of the *Basic Series* booklets or more copies of this book. Consider giving them to serve people in your circles and also to help us share about *ServeNow*.

ServeNow Resources

Basic Series booklets

The 31 booklets are available for purchase individually or in the following five packages from weservenow.org.

Introduction to Christian Faith

Are you looking for a solid explanation about salvation and who God is? In *Introduction to Christian Faith* you learn the basics about Jesus, God, and the Holy Spirit. Additionally, you will find out what it means to be a Christian and what is found in the Bible. It includes the following *Basic Series* booklets:

- *Jesus*
- *Salvation*
- *The Bible*
- *Being a Christian*
- *God*
- *The Holy Spirit*

Foundation for Christian Growth

Need to know how to mature in your faith? In *Foundation for Christian Growth* you are introduced to reading and studying the Bible, taking basics steps for a functioning prayer life, and what church is all about. You will also learn how and why to tell others about your faith, living a godly life in an ever-changing world, and how we can worship God in every aspect of our lives. It includes the following *Basic Series* booklets:

- *Reading and Studying the Bible*
- *Prayer*
- *Church*
- *Sharing Your Faith*
- *Living a Godly Life*
- *Worship*

Develop as Jesus Followers

Do you want to develop as a Jesus follower? Then come to grips with words like *repentance, brokenness, forgiveness, justice, mercy,* and *grace*. Find out how to walk in obedience and faith as well as how to tackle those temptations that all of us struggle with. You will also find that there is more to God's love than you can imagine. It includes the following *Basic Series* booklets:

- *Repentance, Brokenness, and Forgiveness*
- *Obedience*
- *Justice, Mercy , and Grace*
- *Faith*
- *Temptation*
- *God's love*

Serving and Maturity

In *Serving and Maturity* you get inspired and encouraged about how you can serve God, show compassion, and give not just your money, but also your time, talent, and treasure to God. You mature as you learn how to trust God through spiritual warfare, ethical situations in your life as well as facing persecution. It includes the following *Basic Series* booklets:

- *Serving God*
- *Compassion*
- *Spiritual Warfare*
- *Ethics*
- *Giving*
- *Persecution*

Core Knowledge for the Christian

Core Knowledge for the Christian presents basics on love, marriage, and how to raise a family. All of us are familiar with pain and suffering, but how can we understand it? You will be inspired when you realize how God has intervened in the lives of people for 2,000 years and what awaits us in the future. You'll learn what other religions and cults really believe, what God's challenging commission is to all believers as well as how to act when our world falls apart through natural disaster or even pandemics. It includes the following *Basic Series* booklets:

- *Love, Marriage and Family*
- *Pain and Suffering*
- *Heaven and the End Time*
- *World Religion and Cults*
- *The Great Commission*
- *When Our World Falls Apart*
- *God's Intervention in History*

Discussion Questions

Chapter 1

- What situations in life are you going through right now where things are not turning out as you hoped? How are you processing through it? Has it changed your view of God? Are you holding on to anger toward God or unforgiveness toward others? What from this chapter might assist you to work through your perspective?

- Have you found your hope being stirred up in a specific area through this chapter? Perhaps you have lost faith in God because things have not gone as expected? In what ways do you still see God's hand at work in your life or in your heart?

Chapter 2

- Can you identify the kind of hope that is "wishful thinking" versus a confidence inspired by God?

- What areas of life are you worrying about, fearful of, or stressing out about? In what specific ways might you need to anchor your emotions by placing your hope in God?

Chapter 3

- Why do you think there seems to be a corresponding loss of hope as the world improves? How can this be combatted?

- Can you think of a time in your life when you experienced God's love through someone's action on your behalf?

- How can you demonstrate God's goodness in action in someone's life today that could open their hearts to the Good News?

Chapter 4

- In keeping with the prophecy of Joel and the outpouring of the Holy Spirit: What visions from God have you received? What dreams are you dreaming? What passion has God put in your heart? Take some time to pray and ask for the Holy Spirit to help you see what God sees and dream what God dreams!

- What is the next step you can take to see that vision or dream start to become a reality?

- What needs do you see around the world or in your neighborhood? What can you do to start making a difference and meeting one need at a time?

Chapter 5

- What good works do you think Jesus has you here on earth for?

- Are you waking up each day with a sense of "eagerness" to do those good works? Why or why not? If not, commit to praying each day for God to do a work in your heart to create that eagerness.

- If money were not an issue, what would you do to serve others?

Chapter 6

- What do you find helps to restore or renew your hope?

- What can you do this week to put yourself in a position where God can restore or renew your hope?

- Have you been mistaking God's silence for God's absence? Have you been focusing on the "why?" question versus "who?" How can you refocus on God versus circumstances?

Chapter 7

- Have you ever been consumed with shame? How did you overcome it? If battling with it, how can you lay that down today before Jesus who bore your shame on the cross?

- Do you agree or disagree with hopelessness and shame being at the root of suicide? How do you think more awareness and frankness about suicide could be addressed and hope be given to those contemplating it?

Chapter 8

- When was the last time you read any of the Bible personally?

- How can you make sure to build the habit of spending time in God's Word and applying it to your life?

- Can you remember the last time God's Word provided hope to your soul or life? What was the situation, and what was the Scripture that spoke to you?

Chapter 9

- Have you been using your age to limit what God can do in your life or through your life?

- Perhaps your role in life has changed, but how can God use you now in this season of life?

- How can you impart the wisdom God has given you in your age/experiences in life? Whom can you share that wisdom with?

- In what ways is God still working on your character to make you more like Christ? How can you cooperate with him?

- Do you believe your best days are behind you or ahead of you when it comes to God's work in your heart and life?

Chapter 10

- Have you been making the excuse that you are too young for God to use you? Has this chapter served to alter your perspective at all?

- Have you been focused on all you *can't* do or *don't* have versus what you *can* do and what you *do* have?

Chapter 11

- Have you been overcomplicating what it means to serve and obey Jesus? What is he presently telling you to do? What is holding you back from doing it?

- Have you been "waiting" for some miracle to happen versus taking a step of faith trusting that God is in the process?

- To whom can you be a conduit of God's hope this week?

Chapter 12

- What makes you angry? What makes you sad? How can you act on those emotions in a productive way?

- Can you see any area in your life where your anger is misplaced or disproportionate to what God cares about?

- What makes your heart sing? What song has God put in your heart? How are you acting on it?

- When was the last time you lived not by what your physical eyes can see or logical mind make sense of but by the dream in your heart?

Chapter 13

- Have you placed your trust fully in Christ and been born again? If not, why not right now?

- In what specific ways are you participating in the fulfillment of the Great Commission?

Notes

Chapter 1: When All Hope Seems Lost

1. Chad Barrett. *Thrive, Not Just Survive*. Not yet published.
2. Rebecca Joy. Facebook post. August 10, 2020.
3. Attributed to Doghouse Diaries.

Chapter 2: The God of All Hope

1. John Eldredge. *All Things New. Nashville*, TN: Thomas Nelson, 2017, 9.

Chapter 3: As the World Gets Better, People Are Losing Hope

1. UNHCR/Refugee Facts. "Refugee Statistics." Accessed October 14, 2020. https://www.unrefugees.org/refugee-facts/statistics/.
2. Wycliffe Bible Translators. "Our Impact." Accessed October 14, 2020. https://www.wycliffe.org.uk/about/our-impact/.
3. Dan Wooding. "Modern Persecution." May 12, 2010. Christianity.com. https://www.christianity.com/church/church-history/timeline/1901-2000/modern-persecution-11630665.html.
4. Asian Development Bank. "Global Increase in Climate-Related Disasters." November 2015. https://reliefweb.int/sites/reliefweb.int/files/resources/global-increase-climate-related-disasters.pdf.
5. World Health Organization. "World Health Statistics." Accessed October 14, 2020. https://www.who.int/gho/world-health-statistics.

6. United States Department of Health and Human Services. "Human Trafficking Fact Sheet." 2004. https://www.hsdl. org/?abstract&did=23329.

7. Hannah Ritchie, Joe Hasell, Cameron Appel, and Max Roser. "Terrorism." July 2013; revised November 2019. https:// ourworldindata.org/terrorism.

8. Nuclear Threat Initiative (NTI). "The Nuclear Threat." December 21, 2015. https://www.nti.org/learn/nuclear/.

9. Hans Rosling. *Factfulness: Ten Reasons We Are Wrong About the World and Why Things Are Better than You Think.* New York, NY: Flatiron Books, 2018, 3.

10. Ibid., 5.

11. Mark Manson. *Everything Is F*cked: A Book About Hope.* New York, NY: HarperCollins Publishers, 2019, 17.

12. Fareed Zakaria. *The Post-American World | 2.0.* New York: NY: W.W. Norton & Company, 2008, 9.

13. United Nations World Food Program. "COVID-19 will double number of people facing food crises unless swift action is taken." April 21, 2020. https://www.wfp.org/news/covid-19-will-double-number-people-facing-food-crises-unless-swift-action-taken.

14. Jeffrey Gettleman and Suhasini Raj. "As Covid-19 Closes Schools, the World's Children Go to Work." *New York Times,* September 27, 2020. https://www.nytimes.com/2020/09/27/world/asia/covid-19-india-children-school-education-labor.html.

15. Caritas.org. "Cases of Human Trafficking Increase During the COVID-19 Pandemic." July 29, 2020. https://www.caritas.org/2020/07/covid-19-and-human-trafficking/.

16. The World Bank. "COVID-19 to Add as Many as 150 Million Extreme Poor by 2021." October 7, 2020. https://www.worldbank.org/en/news/press-release/2020/10/07/covid-19-to-add-as-many-as-150-million-extreme-poor-by-2021.

17. John Eldredge. *Get Your Life Back*. Nashville, TN: Nelson Books, 2020, xiv.

18. John Eldredge. *All Things New*. Nashville, TN: Thomas Nelson 2017, x.

19. Mark Manson. *Everything Is F*cked: A Book About Hope*. New York, NY: HarperCollins Publishers, 2019, 16.

20. Ibid., 12.

21. Octavio Esqueda. (Blog) "What Every Church Needs to Know About Generation Z." Talbot Magazine, November 14, 2018. https://www.biola.edu/blogs/talbot-magazine/2018/what-every-church-needs-to-know-about-generation-z.

22. Jim Cymbala. *Storm: Hearing Jesus for the Times We Live In*. Grand Rapids, MI: Zondervan, 2014, 28.

Chapter 4: Hope Began with a Toilet

1. Confirmed by letter from Gina A. Zurlo, Ph.D., Center for the Study of Global Christianity, South Hamilton, MA, October 5, 2020.

2. Ibid.

Chapter 5: Hope and a Future

1. John Eldredge. *All Things New*. Nashville, TN: Thomas Nelson 2017, 5.

2. Kimberly McGuane. "With Utz Going Public, Herr's to Become Largest Privately Held Snack Company in Nation."

Vista Today, June 11 2020. https://vista.today/2020/06/
with-utz-going-public-herrs-to-become-largest-privately-
held-snack-company-in-nation.

Chapter 6: Renewing Our Hope

1. Jon Little, "*Behind The Song: Carl Boberg, 'How Great Thou Art.'* " American Songwriter, November 24, 2019. https://
americansongwriter.com/behind-the-song-carl-boberg-how-
great-thou-art/.

2. *One Voice, Hymns for the People of God.* Brentwood, TN: One Voice Publishers, 2026, 8.

3. Philip Yancey. *Where Is God When It Hurts.* Grand Rapids, MI: Zondervan, 1977, 1990, 84.

4. David Goleman. *Emotional Intelligence: Why It Can Matter More than IQ.* London, England: Bloomsbury Publishing, 1995, 6.

5. Matthew Parris quoted in Peter Greer and Chris Horst. *Mission Drift: The Unspoken Crisis Facing Leaders, Charities, and Churches.* Bloomington, MN: Bethany House Publishers, 2014, 35.

6. Ibid., 36.

Chapter 7: Hope in Times of Despair

1. Leo Sher. "The impact of the COVID-19 pandemic on suicide rates." *QJM: An International Journal of Medicine*, Vol. 113, Issue 10, October 2020, 707–712. https://doi.org/10.1093/
qjmed/hcaa202

2. Ians. "Suicide cases on the rise in Nepal during COVID-19 lockdown." *The New Indian Express*, July 7, 2020. https://
www.newindianexpress.com/world/2020/jul/07/suicide-cas-
es-on-the rise-in-nepal-during-covid-19-lockdown.

3. Lea Winernam. "By the Numbers: An Alarming Rate of Suicide." American Psychological Association, January 2019. https://www.apa.org/monitor/2019/01/numbers.

Chapter 8: *The Book Full of Hope*

1. United Bible Societies. "Global Bible Distribution Report: 2017." https://www.unitedbiblesocieties.org/wp-content/uploads/2018/05/RS83897_GSDR-2017_English_final_low-res-spreads.pdf.

2. Adapted from Lawrence Kushner. *Eyes Remade for Wonder.* Woodstock, VT: Jewish Lights Publishing, 1998, 50.

3. Mark Batterson. *Primal: A Quest for the Lost Soul of Christianity.* Colorado Springs, CO: Multnomah Books, 2009, 71.

4. Excerpts from Lars Dunberg. *10 Prescriptions for a Somewhat Sick Church.* Colorado Springs, CO: Mountainbrook Press, 2014, chapter 4.

5. Internal report from Tyndale House Publishers. Published date unknown.

6. Amy Watson. "Bible Readership in the U.S.: 2018-2019." Statista, June 25, 2019. https://www.statista.com/statistics/299433/bible-readership-in-the-usa/.

7. Collin Hansen. "Why Johnny Can't Read the Bible." *Christianity Today*, May 24, 2010. https://www.christianitytoday.com/ct/2010/may/25.38.html.

8. Confidential report.

9. As witnessed by the majority of all Bible organizations during the years after the fall of the Iron curtain in 1989. As late as 1992, Lars Dunberg was personally asked by the Minister of Culture in Russia to provide a Bible for every person in the Moscow White House, approximately 5,000 copies.

Chapter 9: Hope in Our Old Age

1. Daniel Grothe. *Chasing Wisdom*. Nashville, TN: Thomas Nelson: 2020. Kindle Edition, 188.
2. Ed Stetzer. *Christians in the Age of Outrage*. Carol Stream, IL, Tyndale Momentum: 2018, 198.

Chapter 10: Hope for the Young

1. Mary J. Evans. *The Message of Samuel*. Downers Grove, IL: Intervarsity Press, 2004, 110.
2. Mark Batterson. *The Grave Robber: How Jesus Can Make Your Impossible Possible*. Grand Rapids, MI: Baker Publishing Group, 2014, 14.

Chapter 11: Being a Conduit of Hope to Others

1. Source unknown.

Chapter 12: The Ingredients of Hope

1. Homeland Security Digital Database. "Human Trafficking Fact Sheet." United States. Department of Health and Human Services, 2004. https://www.hsdl.org/?abstract&did=23329.
2. Elizabeth Nash and Joerg Dreweke. "The U.S. Abortion Rate Continues to Drop: Once Again, State Abortion Restrictions Are Not the Main Driver." Guttmacher Institute, September 18, 2010; https://www.guttmacher.org/gpr/2019/09/us-abortion-rate-continues-drop-once-again-state-abortion-restrictions-are-not-main.
3. The World Bank. "Poverty: Overview." Last updated October 7, 2020; https://www.worldbank.org/en/topic/poverty/overview?
4. UNHCR.org. "Figures at a Glance." June 18, 2020. https://www.unhcr.org/en-us/figures-at-a-glance.html.

5. American Bible Society. "About." Accessed October 14, 2020. https://american.bible/about-bible-ministry-why-what-where

6. Jacob Westland. "Unreached Peoples: Has Everybody Already Heard the Gospel?" Accessed October 14, 2020. https://www.pioneerseurope.org/en/Stories/Unreached-Peoples.

7. Jim Cymbala. *Storm: Hearing Jesus for the Times We Live In.* Grand Rapids, MI: Zondervan, 2014. 15.

8. Ed Stetzer. *Christians in the Age of Outrage.* Carol Stream, IL: Tyndale House Publishers, 2018, 95.

9. Mark Batterson. *Primal: A Quest for the Lost Soul of Christianity.* Colorado Springs, CO: Multnomah Books, 2009, 2.

10. This line was spoken by Martin Luther King Jr. in a sermon called "Loving Your Enemies," delivered at the Dexter Avenue Baptist Church in Montgomery, Alabama on December 25, 1957.

11. Erwin McManus. *Seizing Your Divine Moment.* Nashville, TN: Thomas Nelson, 2002, 50-51.

12. Kirbyjon Caldwell and Walt Kallestad. *Entrepreneurial Faith: Launching Bold Initiatives to Expand God's Kingdom.* Colorado Springs, CO: Waterbrook Press, 2004, 1.

13. Mark Batterson. *Chase the Lion: If Your Dream Doesn't Scare You, It's Too Small.* Colorado Springs, CO: Multnomah Books, 2016, 3.

14. Oxford Dictionary. https://www.lexico.com/en/definition/dream. Origin: Middle English of Germanic origin, related to Dutch *droom* and German *Traum*, and probably also to Old English *drēam* 'joy, music.'

15. Carmine Gallo. "Steve Jobs: What Makes Your Heart Sing?" Forbes.com. Oct 10, 2011. https://www.forbes.com/sites/

carminegallo/2011/10/10/steve-jobs-what-makes-your-heart-sing/#331e12c94b77.

16. Andy Stanley. *Visioneering: God's Blueprint for Developing and Maintaining Vision.* Colorado Springs, CO. Multnomah Books, 2005, 17.

17. Mark Batterson. *Primal: A Quest for the Lost Soul of Christianity.* Colorado Springs, CO: Multnomah Books, 2009, 112.

18. Ibid., 139.

19. International Movie Database (IMDB). *"Wonder Woman."* *Accessed October 12, 2020.* https://www.imdb.com/title/tt0451279/characters/nm2933757.

20. Bob Roberts. *Glocalization: How Followers of Jesus Engage a Flat World.* Grand Rapids, Michigan: Zondervan, 2007, 95.

21. Erwin McManus. *Seizing Your Divine Moment.* Nashville, TN: Thomas Nelson, 2002, 54-55.

22. Ibid.

Chapter 13: Jesus Christ—the Hope of the World

1. Barna.com. "Research Releases in Faith & Christianity." March 27, 2018. https://www.barna.com/research/half-churchgoers-not-heard-great-commission/.

2. Jim Cymbala. *Storm: Hearing Jesus for the Times We Live In.* Grand Rapids, MI: Zondervan, 2014, 28.

3. Matt Maher. "Alive and Breathing." 2019.

Epilogue

1. NP Source (Nonprofit Source). "Church and Religious Giving Statistics." Accessed October 14, 2020. https://nonprofitssource.com/online-giving-statistics/church-giving/

Bibliography

Barrett, Chad. *Thrive, Not Just Survive.* Not yet published.

Batterson, Mark. *Chase the Lion: If Your Dream Doesn't Scare You, It's Too Small.* Colorado Springs, CO: Multnomah Books, 2016.

Batterson, Mark. *The Grave Robber: How Jesus Can Make Your Impossible Possible.* Grand Rapids, MI: Baker Publishing Group, 2014.

Batterson, Mark. *Primal: A Quest for the Lost Soul of Christianity.* Colorado Springs, CO: Multnomah Books, 2009.

Caldwell, Kirbyjon and Kallestad, Walt. *Entrepreneurial Faith: Launching Bold Initiatives to Expand God's Kingdom.* Colorado Springs, CO: Waterbrook Press, 2004.

Dunberg, Lars B. *Risktaker for God.* Colorado Springs, CO: Global Action, 2008.

Dunberg, Lars B. *10 Prescriptions for a Somewhat Sick Church.* Colorado Springs CO: Mountainbrook Press, 2014.

Dunberg, Lars. *What Bible Should I Read?* Colorado Springs, CO: Global Action, 2006.

Dunberg, Lars. *You Can Change the World.* Colorado Springs, CO: Mountainbrook Press, 2014.

Eldredge, John. *All Things New.* Nashville, TN: Nelson Books, 2017.

Eldredge, John. *Get Your Life Back.* Nashville, TN: Nelson Books, 2020.

Foley, Ben and Dunberg, Lars. *The Basic Things You Need to Know About the Great Commission.* Colorado Springs: *Servenow*, 2020.

Goleman, Daniel. *Emotional Intelligence: Why It Can Matter More than IQ.* London, England: Bloomsbury Publishing, 1995.

Greer, Peter and Horst, Chris. *Mission Drift: The Unspoken Crisis Facing Leaders, Charities, and Churches.* Bloomington, MN: Bethany House Publishers, 2014.

Grothe, Daniel. *Chasing Wisdom*. Nashville, TN: Thomas Nelson: 2020.

Manson, Mark. *Everything Is F*cked: A Book About Hope.* New York, NY: HarperCollins Publishers, 2019.

McManus, Erwin. *Seizing Your Divine Moment.* Nashville, TN: Thomas Nelson, 2002.

Roberts, Bob Jr. *Glocalization: How Followers of Jesus Engage a Flat World.* Grand Rapids, Michigan: Zondervan, 2007.

Rosling, Hans. *Factfulness: Ten Reasons We Are Wrong About the World and Why Things Are Better than You Think.* New York, NY: Flatiron Books, 2018.

Stanley, Andy. *Visioneering: God's Blueprint for Developing and Maintaining Vision.* Colorado Springs, CO. Multnomah Books, 2005.

Stetzer, Ed. *Christians in the Age of Outrage.* Carol Stream, IL: Tyndale House Publishers, 2018.

Yancey, Philip. *Where Is God When It Hurts.* Grand Rapids, MI: Zondervan, 1977, 1990.

Zakaria, Fareed. *The Post-American World 2.0.* New York: NY: W.W. Norton & Company, 2008.